SPORT PSYCHOLOGY LIBRARY:

The Experts Agree:

"Peter Vidmar has done it again. *Sport Psychology: Gymnastics* is a comprehensive guide for athletes, coaches, and parents. This book outlines the philosophy that made Vidmar an Olympic gold medalist and provides the details that can make you a champion both in and out of the gym."

—Bart Conner
NBC Sports Commentator and 1984 Gold Medalist on Pommel Horse

—Nadia Comeneci
Awarded 7 perfect 10s in her multi-gold 1976 Olympic performance

"This book is about the real sport of gymnastics. It's a must-read for every gymnast, coach, parent, and fan. Gymnastics is a very beautiful and physical sport, but few people realize what an important role psychology plays. When faced with adversity, it is your mental strength that will help you come out a winner every time."

—Shannon Miller
Team and individual Gold Medalist, 1996 Olympics

"A practical, interactive book that any gymnast can benefit from. It engages readers so they can actually put the ideas to use."

—Amy Chow
*Member of 1996 Olympic Gold Medal Team
and winner of 1996 Silver Medal on Bars*

"The young reader will be inspired by the stories and examples from their gymnastics heroes and will gain tremendous insight on how to deal with the mental challenges that come with the sport of gymnastics. From the athlete to the parent, this is a wonderful book for anyone involved with gymnastics. Vidmar and Cogan stuck the landing!"

—Tim Daggett
Bronze Medal Winner, Pommel Horse, 1984 Olympics

SPORT PSYCHOLOGY LIBRARY:

GYMNASTICS

Karen D. Cogan
Peter Vidmar

Fitness Information Technology, Inc.
P.O. Box 4425, University Avenue
Morgantown, WV 26504-4425 USA

Library of Congress Card Catalog Number: 99-75650

ISBN 1-885693-17-6

All photos courtesy of the UCLA Athletic Department except the head shot of Peter Vidmar, courtesy of Peter Vidmar, and the photos of Karen Cogan, courtesy of Karen Cogan.

Copyeditor: Sandra R. Woods
Cover Design: James R. Bucheimer
Cover photo: K. Fugiwara
Developmental Editor: Geoffrey C. Fuller
Production Editor: Craig R. Hines
Printed by: Data Reproductions Corporation

Printed in the United States of America
10   9   8   7   6   5   4   3   2   1

Fitness Information Technology, Inc.
P.O. Box 4425, University Avenue
Morgantown, WV 26504 USA
(800) 477-4348
(304) 599-3482
Email: fit@fitinfotech.com
Web Site: www.fitinfotech.com

About the Sport Psychology Library

This book is the second in our Sport Psychology Library series, a unique contribution to the sports world. For the first time ever, sport psychologists and athletes have combined their skills and experience to bring you a series of books that show athletes, coaches, and parents how to get the maximum out of their sports involvement. Each book in the series is focused on a specific sport, so your special needs as a participant in that sport will be directly addressed. I am delighted that the second book in the series is by two outstanding professionals, sport psychologist Karen Cogan and Olympian gymnast Peter Vidmar. Both have extensive experience with gymnastics, and their insights into the sport offer a new perspective on the achievement of excellence.

As Editor-in-Chief of the Sport Psychology Library, I have the privilege of reviewing each book in the library. The result is that while each book in the series stands alone and deals with the factors unique to that sport, the books combine to build an outstanding library of knowledge about the psychology of sport. Expect us to provide two to three books in the Library series each year.

Now, it's time for me to get out of the way, so that you can enjoy this wonderful book!

Shane Murphy, Ph.D.
Editor-in-Chief
Sport Psychology Library

Dr. Shane Murphy is the former head of the Sport Psychology Department of the United States Olympic Committee and is currently President of Gold Medal Psychological Consultants.

About the Authors

Karen Cogan and Peter Vidmar are both former competitive gymnasts and were teammates at UCLA. In 1984, Peter led the U.S. Men's Gymnastics Team to its first-ever Olympic Gold Medal. He also captured the gold on pommel horse, scoring a perfect 10, and won the silver medal in the All-Around competition. In addition, he has numerous NCAA and international titles. Today he translates his skills as a leader and motivator into inspirational presentations for Fortune 500 companies. He also serves on the Executive Committee of USA Gymnastics.

Karen was a competitive gymnast for ten years. Her gymnastics career prematurely ended in college after two serious knee injuries. She then focused her energies on her academic performance and received the UCLA Outstanding Senior Award. She has a master's degree in kinesiology and a Ph.D. in psychology. Now she is a sport psychologist and consults with athletes at the University of North Texas Center for Sport Psychology as well as in her private practice. She is a licensed psychologist, certified sport psychology consultant (CC, AAASP), member of the USA Gymnastics Health Care Providers network, and member of the United States Olympic Committee Sport Psychology Registry.

Table of Contents

List of Exercises

Acknowledgments

We wish to recognize the numerous gymnasts and coaches who have influenced us throughout our gymnastics and professional careers and provided inspiration for writing this book. We also would like to thank Amanda Borden, Tim Daggett, Shannon Miller, Jaycie Phelps, and Kerri Strug for taking the time to participate in the interviews for this project. Their perspectives have been invaluable. In addition, the USA Gymnastics staff provided assistance and information that greatly contributed to the quality of the book.

We appreciate the helpful editorial assistance from the staff at FIT, Shane Murphy, David Feigley, and Sandra Woods, as well as the input from an anonymous reviewer.

Special thanks go to Trent, Kyla, and Braeden Petrie; Bill and Betsy Cogan; Cathy Cogan; and Donna, Timothy, Christopher, Stephen, Kathryn, and Emily Vidmar for their unwavering support throughout this project.

Support for this project was provided by the University of North Texas in granting a development leave for Karen D. Cogan.

INTRODUCTION

1

AN INTRODUCTION TO THE MENTAL SIDE OF GYMNASTICS

One lazy Saturday afternoon, Jill was clicking through channels on the TV. There was auto racing (click), the movie of the week (click), reruns of some old sitcoms (click), . . . and gymnastics. She stopped clicking and was captivated as she watched the young athletes flip and dance through floor routines. Then she watched them swing, twist, and flip through their bar routines. She was watching so intently that she did not even hear her mother come into the room. On the commercial break, she looked up and said, "Mom, I want to do that!" It wasn't long before Jill's parents enrolled her in gymnastics classes, and so started another gymnastics career.

Gymnastics—Watch it once, and you're in awe. Try it once, and you're hooked. Few other sports require the power and grace, strength and beauty, speed and precision, daring and flexibility of gymnastics. Gymnastics' popularity has soared thanks to the impact of the impressive young competitors who grace our television screens, especially during the Olympics. Each year more young athletes choose gymnastics. In fact, approximately 2 million children participate in gymnastics in the United States. Their goals range from a desire to learn some basic gymnastics skills to dreams of competing in the Olympics.

This book gives you practical insights into combining the mental and physical sides of gymnastics. Many gymnasts can learn the physical skills, but those who also can play the mental side of the game will be the most successful. This book will help you learn how to use your mental skills to maximize your gymnastics potential.

Chances are if you have picked up this book, you are a gymnast (or want to be one) or are the parent of a gymnast. This book is geared primarily for competitive gymnasts at the club and collegiate level, but gymnasts of all skill levels can benefit from it. In addition, there are several sections written specifically for parents to help them help their young athletes. Whatever your interest in this wonderful sport, after reading this book you can come away with an understanding of the mental components of gymnastics and how to improve performance through mental training.

Just in case you are skeptical about the role your mind plays in your gymnastics success, here are some thoughts from 1996 Olympic Gold Medalist Amanda Borden: "Gymnastics is a sport that requires a lot of mental toughness. Every elite athlete trains hard. It comes down to [who] is mentally the toughest [and] who can handle the pressure." Jaycie Phelps, another 1996 Olympic Gold Medalist, also discussed using mental skills in her training for the Olympics: "We did a lot of it [visualization in particular]. It was a lot of our success. Most of gymnastics is mental."

There is something so exciting about gymnastics that it's hard to stop once you start. Gymnasts deal with fears and train with minor injuries because the thrill of flying, flipping, and twisting through the air is difficult to match. These athletes work through anxiety and nerves during competitions because the excitement of achieving goals or learning a new skill can be so intense.

When asked to describe the natural high they get from gymnastics, some gymnasts have compared it to a roller-coaster ride at an amusement park. Have you ever gotten on a roller coaster and experienced the exhilaration of that ride? The feeling is incredible, and perhaps you can't wait to get on again. That is what gymnasts experience every day. The only difference is that they rely on their bodies for the thrills rather than on metal and tracks.

Tim Daggett, 1984 Olympic Gold Medalist, discussed how he became interested in gymnastics:

> I loved the feeling of height, climbing, flying, moving fast. As I got older it became fun to test myself and challenge myself. I also learned about life. I have no idea what I would be professionally and personally [without gymnastics] because everything has been impacted by this. I take what I learned from the gym—work hard, be dedicated, sacrifice—and everything will eventually be OK. It has to do with the struggle.

Fans also are drawn to this sport that defies gravity and nerves (and teaches life lessons). Over the past decade, gymnastics has evolved and now includes more and more spectacular and original moves. Highly trained competitors make their movements look easy and effortless, but anyone who has ever tried those moves finds it takes hours of work to reach even a small degree of perfection. So if you can't experience the thrill of throwing your own body in the air, it can be exciting just to watch someone else do it. Whether your interest in gymnastics is as an athlete, coach, parent, or fan, this book will show you how the mind and body can work together to produce excellence in this fascinating sport.

Throughout the book, authors Karen Cogan and Peter Vidmar share some of their own experiences as gymnasts and insights into achieving performance excellence. In addition, as part of the research for this book, Peter and Karen had the privilege of interviewing successful past Olympians, Amanda Borden, Tim Daggett, Shannon Miller, Jaycie Phelps, and Kerri Strug, about their experiences. Written answers to several questions were provided by Amanda (12/1/97), Shannon (11/21/97), Jaycie (12/2/97), and Kerri (11/25/97). Amanda and Jaycie offered additional information in follow-up telephone interviews on 12/10/97 and 12/19/97, respectively. Tim Daggett participated in a telephone interview on 12/4/97 to address the interview questions. These interviews are the sources of the quotations and information you will find about these athletes throughout the book. All the gymnasts gave permission for their information to be included here.

Mitch Gaylord, UCLA gymnast and 1984 Olympic Gold Medalist

GETTING STARTED: LEARNING THE BASICS IN GYMNASTICS

To start off, you need to understand the basics, both physical and mental, of the sport. Keep in mind that basic skills are not necessarily easy skills. For instance, holding a hollow-body handstand might at first seem easy, but doing it correctly is a real challenge. Basics involve body awareness, learning to fall safely, and the ability to change your body position in the middle of performing a complicated skill (e.g., changing from arch to hollow position while swinging on uneven bars or high bar). Your mental training also consists of basics that are outlined below. Take the time to invest in the physical and mental basics, and give yourself the foundation you will need later.

The Basic Physical Skills

Women's gymnastics. Women's gymnastics is composed of four events: vault, uneven parallel bars (bars), balance beam

(beam), and floor exercise (floor). Gymnasts who compete on all four events in a single meet are considered All-Around competitors. When a gymnast performs a routine in a meet, her performance is evaluated by judges (two at the local level, four at the national level, and six at the international level). Each judge gives her a score that ranges from 0.00 to 10.00, with 10.00 being a perfect performance. Every gymnast dreams of achieving that perfect 10.00, but only a few of the best in the world ever achieve that perfection. If only two judges are assigning scores, the two scores are averaged for the gymnast's final score. At major competitions, four to six judges are used for each piece of apparatus, and these judges deduct for execution and composition. With four or six judges, the lowest and highest scores are eliminated and the middle ones are averaged. Two other judges determine the *start values* based on the difficulty of the routine. *Start values* are the highest possible score attainable given the overall difficulty of a gymnastics routine, and many routines start lower than a 10.00.

Men's gymnastics. Men's gymnastics is composed of six events: floor exercise (floor), parallel bars, high bar, pommel horse, rings, and vault. As with women's gymnastics, those who compete on all six events in a meet are All-Around competitors. Men are judged using a scoring system that is similar to the women's.

The Basics of Your Gymnastics Attitude

Now let's consider some general attitudes that will help you be successful in gymnastics.

Be patient. When you are getting started in gymnastics, it might be tempting to skip the easy skills (the basics) and move right into the exciting, spectacular moves. But don't rush. You will find that patience pays off. Think of it like a pyramid that has a big foundation and can be built higher from there. If you took away the foundation, all of the top stones would come tumbling down. So learn your basics. Do simple moves, like a forward roll, with good form and flair . . . and do them well every time. Do the same with your handstands. A handstand is probably the single most important element in gymnastics because you use it in some form on every event. Make every handstand count.

Practice makes permanent. You've probably heard that "practice makes perfect," and many athletes try to live up to that standard. More important, practice makes PERMANENT. What you practice is what you compete. Don't expect to train halfheartedly in the gym and then give near-flawless performances in meets because of the extra adrenaline rush. And don't practice with bent knees and flexed toes and expect to miraculously come away with straight legs and pointed toes when you compete. When you are dealing with the pressures of competition, you don't have time to think, and any habits (good or bad) you've developed will kick in. So if you have been doing skills correctly in the gym, you have a much better chance of doing them correctly when you have additional competition pressures to worry about. Learn skills the right way from the start, and make practice count.

Be safe. We all know gymnastics, as well as other physical activities, poses the risk of accidental injury, but sometimes injuries occur needlessly. A mat is crooked or a cable is not tight enough, and you are so intent on doing gymnastics that you don't want to take any extra time away from training. It takes two seconds to kick a mat into place. It takes months to rehabilitate torn ligaments. Sometimes a single needless injury can plague a gymnast for the rest of his or her gymnastics career. So always take those few extra minutes to ensure your safety and that of your teammates.

In addition, now there is a safety certification program that is administered through USA Gymnastics, the national governing body of gymnastics in the United States. Safety certification is required for all coaches and officials on the floor at state-level competitions or above in men's, women's, and rhythmic gymnastics programs. The goal of the safety program is to reduce the number and severity of injuries in gymnastics. Safety certification is recognized and expected of coaches and other gymnastics personnel in the gymnastics community. Check with your coach to make sure he or she has gone through the certification program.

Now that you know some basics about the sport, both physical and mental, let's take a look at the environment in which gymnasts live and train.

THE GYMNASTICS ENVIRONMENT

To adequately understand the mental side of gymnastics, you must also be aware of the environment in which gymnasts train and compete. The gymnastics environment is unique, and it shapes how gymnasts respond to and cope with any challenges they face.

Women's gymnastics. For women, training usually begins at a young age, sometimes as young as 5 years old. Some gymnasts may enjoy the sport because of the sensation of learning new movements, but choose not to put the time and commitment into competing. That's fine. Others may choose to compete and make their way through USA Gymnastics Levels 1–10 and elite. Levels 1–4 are noncompeting levels, although in some states girls at Level 4 can compete. At Levels 5–6, gymnasts compete with compulsories and can progress to the state championship level. Level 7 is a combination of compulsories and optionals, although the optionals have certain specific requirements. At Levels 8–10 and Elite, gymnasts compete in optionals only. Elite is the highest level a gymnast can achieve and is the level from which National and Olympic team members are selected.

Because girls reach their gymnastics peak at a young age, intensive preparation and training in the early years become important if a gymnast is to achieve her goals. If the gymnast chooses to be a serious competitor and devotes herself to the sport, by the age of 12 or 13, she may be spending twenty to thirty hours per week in the gym. Those who train for the Olympics can spend up to forty hours a week in the gym. At this point, it becomes easy to eat, drink, talk, sleep, and live gymnastics. Often many of the gymnast's social activities center on the sport and her teammates, and she has probably given up other activities to have time for gym.

Some gymnasts who have Olympic or world-class aspirations even move away from home to train in high-level gyms with well-known coaches in hopes of reaching their goals. Parents and families often sacrifice a great deal for this type of training. The cost of this training may require parents to put much of their earnings into the sport. The location of a good gym may require giving up family time because one parent must relocate with the gymnast. Other gymnasts may train just as intensely, but are able to stay close to home. Even training close to home can require sacrifices from a family, such as training costs, driving to the gym, and giving up family meals.

Some gymnasts may work toward competing in college. Many college teams recruit former Olympians or world-class athletes, but lesser known gymnasts (often Level 9 or 10) also are recruited by universities and successfully reach their prime in their college years. Even making a college team, however, is becoming more and more competitive.

Team or individual sport? When a gymnast first begins competing in the USA Gymnastics system, she usually trains with a team. Often there are many gymnasts at different skill levels who train together as they work toward competing during the season. Unlike sports such as basketball or soccer, gymnasts are not required to work together to reach a goal. One athlete's performance does not affect a teammate's score. So, despite the team training atmosphere, gymnastics is generally considered an individual sport in which gymnasts compete for indi-

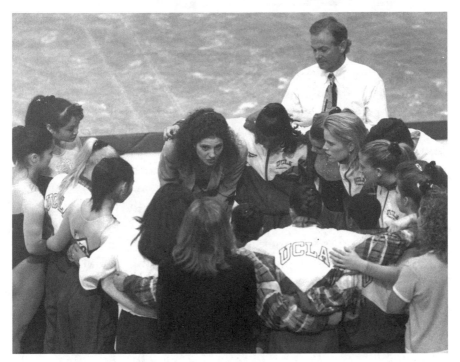

UCLA Team Huddle, Western Regionals, April 1996

vidual honors. Although there are some selected team competitions, such as the Olympic Team Finals and various other invitationals, a gymnast is usually recognized for what she individually accomplishes. This type of environment can create competition between teammates.

It is common to view gymnastics as an individual sport, but if you spend three to six hours a day in the gym with your teammates, you must get along. Supporting and helping your teammates will make all of you better performers in the long run, and if you want help, you also have to learn to give help. You go through difficult as well as joyful times with your teammates, who may very well become lifelong friends.

A team focus is especially important if you plan to compete in college. At the college level, the primary focus becomes the team achievements. Although individual achievements are recognized, these achievements are secondary to those of the team. Collegiate coaches emphasize team support and encourage the gymnasts to "do what is best for the team" rather than strive only for personal goals. Gymnasts often have difficulty rapidly adjusting their attitudes to accept this new team-centered approach after many years as individual competitors.

Another team aspect of collegiate gymnastics to which a gymnast must adjust is the competition procedure. In Olympic and National competitions, each gymnast who qualifies for a given meet must be an All-Around competitor. By contrast, in collegiate competitions, each team performs only six routines on each event. The team may consist of twelve to fifteen gymnasts, and not all the gymnasts can compete on every event in each meet. Some members of a team may specialize in only one or two events or may not compete at all. All athletes are vying for the top six spots on each event, while simultaneously the coaches are encouraging them to be team oriented and supportive of each other. Gymnasts often experience mixed feelings in that they want what is best for the team, but also wish to achieve their own personal goals. The changes in competition procedures and the new focus on the team can contribute to a lack of cohesiveness in the environment. If gymnasts begin training with a "team attitude" early in their careers, the transition to college can be made more smoothly. For instance, gymnasts can learn to genuinely support each other during workouts and meets, whatever the outcome. Learning to gracefully accept your own wins as well as those of your teammates will create a positive team atmosphere. Additionally, although the competitive spirit will always be present in the gym or on the competition floor, you can develop a healthy respect for those who are more successful than you while increasing your own ambition to achieve.

Men's gymnastics. For men the same type of environment exists, although intensive training for men may begin at a slightly older age. To be successful, men need physical strength that they generally do not develop until they reach adolescence. The top junior boys, though, still may be training twenty hours a week by age 14. College gymnastics is often different for men too. At this level many of the top male gymnasts are just reaching their prime and are training for international and Olympic competitions. They all work for team success, but some also must diligently focus on their personal goals. In the right environment the gymnast can accomplish both goals without sacrificing one or the other.

Men may also experience the additional pressures of what might seem like two competitive seasons superimposed on top of each other. They compete in the collegiate meets and are also participating in additional national or international meets outside of the college season. Sometimes they must "peak" more than once throughout the year.

After reading this, you might be thinking, "Wow! This sport is a huge commitment." Well, it is if your goals are to compete nationally, collegiately, or internationally. But there are many other ways to participate in gymnastics at lower levels of intensity. You may choose to take classes at a local gym or YMCA. Or you may want to compete only for your high school team. These types of programs give gymnasts the opportunity to learn and progress without the time commitment and pressures of highly competitive training. So choose the environment that meets your needs.

If you are a gymnast (or the parent of one) who chooses more intense training, you might also be wondering how to handle the pressures associated with such training. There is quite a bit of discussion about whether such young athletes should be subjected to such pressures. The choice to pursue a competitive sport (and the associated pressures) is a personal one with each gymnast and family having different goals, needs, and tolerance of pressure. Parents will want to balance providing their children with opportunities and at the same time protecting them from high demands and pressures. Many parents help their athletes successfully manage and reduce the pressures involved. Throughout this book, and especially in chapter 5, you will find suggestions and strategies for managing the demands placed upon young gymnasts. It is important for young gymnasts at the most competitive levels to keep things in perspective, stay healthy, reduce pressures, and feel happy.

The gymnastics environment shapes how gymnasts learn and cope with challenges. With an understanding of the environment, you can better appreciate the important mental abilities necessary for training and competing in gymnastics. The next chapter outlines the mental side of gymnastics.

THE
SPORT
PSYCHOLOGY
OF
GYMNASTICS

4

PLAYING THE MENTAL GAME OF GYMNASTICS

During the 1996 Olympics, the U.S.A. Women's gymnastics team made history. The team had performed exceptionally well prior to their last event, vault. It looked as if these young women would win the team competition . . . as long as they made it through vault. The first competitors landed their vaults, and confidence was building. Then Dominique Moceanu surprisingly fell on both vaults. This was not a problem because the lowest score is dropped in the team competition. But Kerri Strug also fell on her first vault and appeared to have injured her foot as she walked back to the beginning of the runway. Everyone was shocked, and the tension was building. Now victory was no longer a certainty. There was some confusion about whether a solid vault was needed from Kerri to pull off a win so she vaulted again despite some pain. She landed the vault solidly but severely injured her foot in the process. Kerri literally vaulted into fame as the women went on to win the team gold for the first time ever.

What a mixture of emotions and reactions during the last moments of that vault rotation! Confidence, fear, anxiety, confusion, elation, and concern, to name a few. And what an outstanding example of the psychological processes at work—performing under pressure, competing while in pain, and dealing with the crowd and fans.

Many athletes have the physical abilities to perform difficult and complicated gymnastics skills, but gymnastics also is a mental sport. In fact, some believe sport is 100% physical and 100% mental! That means in addition to physical abilities, a gymnast's performance is based on the ability to concentrate, focus, maintain intensity, and feel positive about oneself. These abilities are known as mental toughness. When the pressure is on, mental toughness separates the superior gymnasts from the good ones.

You might understand how mental toughness plays a role in high-level competition such as the Olympics, but don't forget that it also affects everyday workouts and less pressure-filled competitions. Mental toughness helps gymnasts get around their fears and go for everything they are capable of doing. For example, when learning a new skill, a gymnast might do it perfectly when the coach is spotting or standing near by, but when the coach steps away, the athlete won't go for it and is literally paralyzed by his mind. Or in practice a gymnast might be able to stay on the beam and perform a steady, solid routine, but in competition, she is shaking and falls; she is unable to perform the routine just as she does in practice.

Examples of the mental side of gymnastics are abundant. You can't separate yourself from your mind; it's going to be there influencing your performance one way or another. So you can either let it take over, or train it to help you achieve excellence in gymnastics. Before you read further in this book, try the self-assessment Exercise 4-1.

4-1: SELF-ASSESSMENT

How do you play the mental gymnastics game?

For each question, circle the appropriate number on the scale below. The number(s) in parentheses after each question refer to the chapter in the book that will help you in that area.

1. How often do you say negative things to yourself about your gymnastics? (7)

Most of the time		Sometimes		Almost never
1	2	3	4	5

2. How often do you get so frustrated with your performances that your practices become unproductive? (7)

Most of the time		Sometimes		Almost never
1	2	3	4	5

3. How easily do you block out distractions in the gym so you can concentrate on your routines? (8)

Very difficult		Somewhat easily		Very easily
1	2	3	4	5

4. How easily can you visualize or imagine yourself performing your routines flawlessly? (6)

Very difficult		Somewhat easily		Very easily
1	2	3	4	5

5. How successfully do you handle competitive anxiety and pressure? (5)

Not at all successfully		Somewhat		Very successfully
1	2	3	4	5

6. How excited are you about going to the gym every day? (7, 28)

Not at all excited		Somewhat excited		Very excited
1	2	3	4	5

7. How willing are you to keep working when you are physically tired? (5)

Not at all		Somewhat		Very much
1	2	3	4	5

8. How well do you communicate with your coaches? (21)

Not well		Somewhat well		Very well
1	2	3	4	5

9. How much do you allow a bad performance on one skill or event to pull you down for the next skill or event? (7, 8, 23)

Very much		Somewhat		Not at all
1	2	3	4	5

10. How often do you set goals to help you achieve what you want in gymnastics? (9)

Hardly ever		Sometimes		Almost always

If most of your answers are "5," then you probably already have developed a number of useful mental skills. This book can help you maintain what you have learned as well as develop even more skills. If most of your answers are "1," then

Jill Andrews, UCLA gymnast

you will probably find the mental training skills in this book to be very useful. If, like most people, your answers range in between, then you likely have developed some mental skills but can still learn more. Look at how you answered specific questions to determine where you need work. Wherever you are in your self-assessment, read on. Chances are this book can help you improve your mental skills.

The items to which you responded in the self-assessment are all related to sport psychology skills. In general, sport psychology is concerned with how your thinking affects your physical performance. Sport psychology skills help you learn to be mentally tough when the pressure is on.

Sport psychology training is not magical; practicing mental skills a few times does not automatically make you an outstanding or mentally tough athlete. Think about your mental training as you would your physical training. You spend countless hours learning physical skills and practicing tricks and routines. You would not expect to give Shannon Miller's 1996 Olympic beam performance if you take gymnastics lessons only three times a week. You wouldn't be able to win rings consistently over the past several years as Yuri Chechi has if you had never even done a routine in practice. Likewise, it takes practice to learn mental skills. The more you practice mental skills, the more mentally prepared you become, and the more these skills can help you in difficult situations. Mental training is important and can easily be incorporated into your practice schedule.

We have been talking about mental training in a very general sense up to this point, and you may be wondering what types of mental skills we are talking about. Next we will discuss basic mental strategies, which include relaxation, energizing, positive thinking, visualization, concentration strategies, and goal setting. In the following chapters, we will examine how these skills can be used for each gymnastics event.

LEARNING TO PSYCH UP OR CALM DOWN: USING RELAXATION AND ENERGIZING STRATEGIES

Before reading this chapter do self-assessment 5-1 on the next page.

5-1: SELF-ASSESSMENT

How much do you experience each of the following when doing gymnastics?

a. sweating hands

Not at all		Somewhat		Very much
1	2	3	4	5

b. rapidly beating heart (when not exerting yourself)

Not at all		Somewhat		Very much
1	2	3	4	5

c. butterflies or tension in your stomach (even nausea)

Not at all		Somewhat		Very much
1	2	3	4	5

d. tension in your body (such as muscle tension)

Not at all		Somewhat		Very much
1	2	3	4	5

e. shaky or jittery feelings

Not at all		Somewhat		Very much
1	2	3	4	5

f. negative thinking about yourself or your abilities

Not at all		Somewhat		Very much
1	2	3	4	5

g. worries about performing poorly in workout

Not at all		Somewhat		Very much
1	2	3	4	5

h. worries about not doing well in competition

Not at all		Somewhat		Very much
1	2	3	4	5

i. worries that others will be disappointed in you

Not at all		Somewhat		Very much
1	2	3	4	5

All these feelings and thoughts are indications of anxiety or nervousness and are common experiences in gymnastics, especially prior to competitions. This chapter shows you how to handle any of the above feelings so that they don't interfere with your performance. First, let's look at how two gymnasts experience anxiety when training or competing.

Jennifer. At the beginning of bar practice that day, Jennifer's coach told the gymnasts that he would require them all to make one routine without a major error before moving on to the next event. He also mentioned that if it took until the end of workout, they would each do one successful routine. Jennifer began to feel nervous. Her Delchev (release move) had been very inconsistent, and she was afraid that she would be stuck on bars for the rest of workout. Besides, her hands were already sore from the day before, and she could barely envision her usual bar workout, let alone a whole day there. She walked over to the chalk box thinking she needed a miracle.

Brittany. It was the last rotation of the meet. Brittany was trying to qualify for Nationals, and she knew that she did not have a chance unless she hit this beam routine. Beam had always been her worst event, and she had not hit one flip-flop layout in warm-ups. In fact, she was not feeling at all confident about sticking her beam routine. If she did not stick it, she could forget about going to Nationals. The more she thought about this, the more her hands began to sweat and the shakier she was. She felt butterflies in her stomach, and her heart started racing. She even began to feel nauseated.

Brittany and Jennifer circled lots of "5"s on their self-assessments. It probably did not take long for them to recognize anxiety when they felt it in those pressured situations. There is no question that gymnastics is a high-anxiety sport. It's rare to find a gymnast who doesn't face regular anxiety. Training itself can create chronic anxiety because gymnasts are constantly expected to try harder, more difficult moves and, in doing so, risk injury. Then add competition on top of that, and you get a double dose of anxiety. Also, don't forget other pressures, such as school, personal, or home problems, conflicts with teammates, and expectations from coaches or family. Anxiety can contribute to poor performance, lack of enjoyment in the sport, dropping out of the sport, and a sense of constantly being on edge.

What is anxiety exactly? Because learning any gymnastics skill involves starting with the basics, let's do the same with understanding anxiety. First, we'll need to forget about anxiety for a moment and think about the more neutral term, *activation*.

Here are some basics about how our bodies get activated. We all have some level of energy or activation in our bodies all the time. We have to have some muscle tension, for example, or we would fall down when we stood up. Depending on what you are doing, your body can be more or less activated. For instance, if you are lying down resting, you are at a low activation level, but if you are running down the runway to vault, you are exerting a much higher level of energy. The level of activation is not a positive or negative thing—it merely describes your current energy level.

It is important to remember that different skills require different levels of activation. For your best beam performance, you will want a more reduced activation level so you can remain steady. But on vault you'll probably want a high level of activation for a powerful approach to the horse.

Different gymnasts require different levels of activation, too. Some gymnasts may constantly be in a hyper state and need to bring their activation level down. Others may have difficulty "getting up" for a routine and need to further energize. The important point to remember is that for every gymnast performing every skill, there is a personal, optimal level of activation that will help him or her perform the best. You need to find the level that works best for you.

It will be easier to understand how activation works if you look at the following graph (Fig. 1). We call this graph the "inverted-U." For the best performance, you want to find your personal, moderate level that will land you on the top of the curve.

Here's where anxiety comes into play. Your activation level can take on different meanings depending on how you think about it. For example, if your body feels activated and you are worried or scared, you are likely to decide that you feel anxious or stressed. Anxiety or stress can pull you down and make you less productive. But if your body is activated and you are anticipating something good (like your birthday or a fun vacation), you will probably decide that you are excited. This excitement can be used to your benefit. So whether you are anxious or excited depends on how you think about it, and you

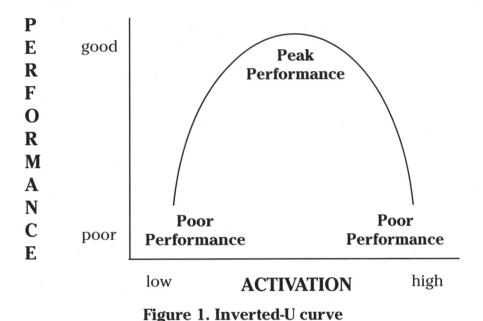

Figure 1. Inverted-U curve

can learn to shift your thinking to view your activation more positively.

You can feel anxiety in two ways, in your body and in your mind. In your body, you feel the physical sensations of anxiety including butterflies in your stomach, sweaty palms, stomach-ache, nausea, and general tension. Check Exercise 5-1 (items a, b, c, d, and e) to see how you rated yourself on these physical signs of anxiety. You also can feel it in your mind through what you tell yourself about the consequences of a performance. Check items f, g, h, and i to see how you rated yourself on these mental signs of anxiety. As you look at your answers, keep in mind that you can be high on physical anxiety, mental anxiety, or both. Knowing how you experience anxiety will help you determine which strategies (presented in the next section of this chapter) to use to control it.

Gymnastics is famous for producing anxiety and stress. New skills can be difficult to learn, and competitions can be intense. You can't always get rid of that uncomfortable anxious feeling by telling yourself that it is really excitement. The key is to learn to work with anxiety rather than avoid it. You want to control your anxiety and activation, not let them control you. Many gymnasts even believe they need a certain amount of anxiety to perform their best.

Tim Daggett (1984 Olympic Gold Medalist–Team) discussed anxiety in this way:

> I don't believe you can truly relax or that you should try to. . . . You need to feel anxiety. It is a normal thing. If you focus too much on relaxing, you won't do what is needed. I learned to work with it, not against it. I would have anxiety one month before a competition. I needed it to go completely out.

Shannon Miller also finds some anxiety helpful. "I also enjoy some of the nerves before a meet. For me it tells me that I still enjoy competition and I still want to go out there and give it my all."

Strategies for Controlling Anxiety

We all know that too much tension or anxiety is uncomfortable. So all you have to do is just relax, right? Anyone who has ever tried that knows it is not always so easy to turn off the anxiety, especially in a high-pressure situation, but there are strategies you can use to help yourself cope with anxiety. First, decide if there is any way to eliminate the source of your anxiety. This strategy only works only if the thing causing you anxiety is not a priority for you. For instance, you might feel stress because you do not have enough time in the day for school, practice, family, and a social life. If you take a look at all your commitments, you might decide that being in the Spanish club at school takes too much time and is not a priority for you. Therefore, you might decide to stop participating in the club to free up some extra time and reduce your stress level.

It is also helpful to examine what you can and cannot control in your life. For instance, gymnasts cannot control their coach's or teammate's behaviors, the judges' subjective impressions, or their placement in the competition lineup, but often gymnasts become anxious about these types of things and spend energy worrying about them. Unfortunately, worrying only distracts you from what you need to do and doesn't get you far. Instead, focus on the things you can control. Then you are focusing on the factors that you can change, and you have more opportunities to control your success.

You can control what you do to prepare for stress. You can teach your body how to reduce anxiety (although you probably won't lose it completely) by learning relaxation exercises. Relaxation exercises work best when you make them a part of your training routine. Remember that practice makes permanent. The more time and effort you put into learning to quickly relax, the more effectively you will be able to relax when you need to the most. There are many relaxation strategies you can use, but the following are some that work well with gymnastics.

When you feel physical anxiety (e.g., sweaty palms, butterflies in the stomach), physical relaxation strategies are the most useful. Check your responses to items a, b, c, d, and e of Exercise 5-1 to determine your level of physical anxiety. If you respond with high scores on any of these items, you have a tendency toward physical anxiety. Deep breathing, progressive muscle relaxation, and cue-controlled relaxation are some popular strategies to control physical anxiety.

Deep breathing. The simplest and quickest exercise is deep breathing. Taking a few deep breaths can quickly bring your anxiety levels down. Shannon Miller endorses breathing skills as an anxiety reducer and says, "Remembering to breathe is always helpful." With every exhale, you release tension. But this is just the first step. To really master relaxation, you will want to practice more involved relaxation techniques. To integrate relaxation training more completely into your mental preparation routine, learn and consistently practice one or more of the following.

Progressive muscle relaxation (PMR). PMR involves systematically tensing and relaxing groups of muscles throughout the body. Typically, you start with your hands and arms, move to your head and body, and then your legs and feet. In this way, you start to feel the difference between tension and relaxation and can more easily choose the "relax" option when needed.

Exercise 5-2 is a sample practice exercise that can assist you in learning PMR. You can use it in a couple of ways:

1. You can read it into a tape recorder and then use it when you have a chance to close your eyes in a relaxed state. Remember to leave pauses in between muscle groups so you have enough time to tense and relax.

2. You can memorize it after reading through it a few times and use it any time you wish.

5-2: LEARN PMR

Get into a comfortable position (for example, lying down with your clothing loosened). Begin breathing deeply, and then close your eyes. Continue to breathe deeply, releasing tension every time you exhale. Allow any tension to leave your body and any concerns about your day to leave your mind. Now focus on the muscles of your right arm. Tense those muscles as much as you comfortably can for 5 seconds. Now release the tension and allow your right arm to relax for approximately 45 seconds. Tense the muscles of your right arm again for 5 seconds and release for 45 seconds. Notice the contrast between being tense and being relaxed. Now focus on the muscles of your left arm and tense for 5 seconds, release for 45 seconds, tense for 5 seconds, and release for 45 seconds. Again, notice how it feels for those muscles to become very relaxed. Now alternate tensing and relaxing (tense [5 seconds], relax [45 seconds], tense [5 seconds], relax [45 seconds]) as you did with your arms for the following muscle groups: (a) face area, (b) neck, (c) torso (upper body), (d) right leg, and (e) left leg. After you have proceeded through all muscle groups, scan your body to see if any tension remains. If you notice tension anywhere, make note of it, and let it go. Stay in this state of relaxation for several minutes, and recognize how your muscles feel to be this relaxed. Remember that you can return to this state as needed in the future. When you are ready, slowly bring yourself out of the relaxed state by (a) moving your fingers and toes, (b) moving your arms and legs, (c) moving your head and neck, and (d) opening your eyes.

Cue-controlled relaxation (CCR). CCR is an extension of PMR. With this method you learn PMR first. Then you choose a relaxing cue word. Many people choose "calm" or "relax" or some other similar word. You begin your session by progressing through the tense/relax phase for each muscle group. Once you have become completely relaxed, you focus on your steady breathing. You then begin saying the cue word to yourself every time you exhale for approximately one minute. You stop saying your cue word for approximately two minutes and enjoy the relaxed state. Then begin repeating your cue word on each exhale for another minute. You will need to practice this exercise every day for several weeks for maximum benefit. In the future, when you feel tense, you simply repeat your cue word and can more easily let go of the tension.

Mental Relaxation

Sometimes your mind is the source of the anxiety. Check items f, g, h, and i in Exercise 5-1 to determine your level of mental anxiety. If you scored high on any of these items, then your mind (rather than body) needs to relax.

Thought stopping. Sometimes you can talk yourself into feeling anxious because of the things you say to yourself. Karen Cogan has heard gymnasts say, "It's my first time at Nationals, and everyone else looks so good. I can't possibly compete with them. And beam has not been going well; I'll probably fall. I can't do this." These types of thoughts increase anxiety. If you hear yourself saying these types of things, the next thing out of your mouth (or in your head) should be the word "STOP!" Take a deep breath, and then start doing some thought replacement as outlined below.

Thought replacement. It might be easy to tell yourself to stop thinking negative, unproductive thoughts, but keeping those thoughts out of your head is another story. The minute you say, "Don't think about falling," what happens? You think about falling. So you need to put something in place of that thought.

Instead try "It's my first Nationals, and I've trained hard to get here. I can compete with the best of them. I may have been having trouble on beam, but all I have to do is stay calm and focused. I've hit this routine hundreds of times before and I can do it now. I can be calm and focused." If you think, "I'm afraid I'll get hurt on my double full," try "Just focus on a good take-off. I know what to do, and I've done it hundreds of times into the pit." If you find yourself saying, "I'm too tired to make it through this floor exercise routine," think "Go hard, stay energized, push through to the end" instead. These replacement thoughts are much more productive and calming than negative ones and get you focused on what you need to do.

Many gymnasts experience anxiety both physically and mentally. When that is the case, you need to relax both the mind and body. One relaxation strategy that does both is meditation.

Meditation. Meditation has four requirements:

1. A quiet place.

2. A comfortable position. Often athletes choose a relaxed state as part of their comfortable position.

3. A mental device that is used to focus on something non-stimulating. This could be a mantra, which is a meaningless, rhythmic sound of one or two syllables that can be repeated over and over during the meditation. Some athletes, for instance, have chosen the syllable *one* or *ohm*. The important thing is to pick a syllable that works for you. Instead of a word, the mental device could be an object to gaze at during meditation.

4. A passive attitude. Gymnasts should not worry about how they are performing during meditation, but should just let it happen as it does. Distractions are to be expected, especially at first, and the gymnast must simply redirect her attention back to the meditation. Try Exercise 5-3 to begin learning meditation.

5-3: MEDITATION

After you are quiet and comfortable, begin breathing steadily and focus on your breathing. With each exhale repeat your mantra. If your mind wanders, bring it back and focus on your breathing. Continue breathing and repeating your mantra for fifteen to twenty minutes at a time. Practice at least once daily.

Some quick and simple ideas from champions. Some gymnasts might find relief from excess anxiety with these other quick strategies that have been suggested by former Olympians. Distraction can be effective in reducing anxiety and has been used by the best. For instance, while she is waiting to compete, Amanda Borden tries to keep her mind on other things, such as reading, playing games, or watching movies. Jaycie Phelps might listen to music or watch movies prior to competition. In addition, others rely on spiritual beliefs. Shannon Miller says, "Trusting in God to help me through is the best way for me to calm my nerves."

Now think back to Brittany's and Jennifer's anxiety that was described at the beginning of this chapter. Both of them felt some mental anxiety (began to think about worst outcomes) and some physical anxiety (butterflies, nervousness), but Brittany and Jennifer had training in applying relaxation strategies to counteract their anxiety. The first thing each of them did was to take a few deep breaths. Jennifer then told herself to stop thinking about missing her Delchev and to focus on what it felt like during the times she had made it. She told herself, "I know what to do and I've made it before. I can hit the first routine." Brittany had been practicing cue-controlled relaxation, and when she realized she was overanxious, she began to repeat "calm" to herself on each exhale. She was able to reduce her anxiety so that she could focus on hitting a nearly flawless beam routine.

Energizing. In contrast to the anxious gymnast is the one who feels too relaxed or too exhausted to practice or compete. Although gymnasts might encounter this problem less than anxiety overload, it can be just as frustrating. So instead of relaxing, you must energize.

Sometimes you've got to get "up" for a workout, and instead you feel exhausted. Or maybe you have been sitting for a while waiting for your turn to vault during a meet. All of a sudden you realize you are next up, and you feel cold and stiff. In these types of situations, you know you need something, and it's not relaxation. You need some energy instead.

One way to energize is through breathing. You can energize by taking deep, pumped-up breaths. Perhaps you have seen weight lifters do that just before they lift. First, begin breathing deeply with a regular, relaxed rhythm. Then increase your rhythm, and with each exhale, imagine that you are producing more and more energy. With each inhale, think "energy in," and with each exhale think "fatigue out." You also can use energizing imagery. As you perform your energized breathing, you might imagine an "energy bolt" coursing through your body, or you might imagine your muscles becoming stronger and putting forth power.

In addition, you might want to choose some energy-inducing cue words to help you in situations where you need to psych up fast. Pick a word or two that helps get you quickly into an energized state. For instance, gymnasts might choose words like "fast," "explode," "go," or "push." You can experiment until you find a word that helps you think and feel energy. Use Exercise 5-4 to help you incorporate cue words into your training.

5-4: ENERGIZING WORDS

1. Pick a word that energizes you (e.g., "go," "push," or "fast").
2. Close your eyes and focus on your breathing. Begin taking a few energizing breaths.
3. With each exhale, say your cue word.
4. Do this for a minute. Be sure to stop if you feel yourself beginning to hyperventilate.
5. After one minute, stop repeating your cue word and focus on how your body feels in this relaxed state for a few minutes.
6. Repeat your cue word again on each exhale for one minute.

Some gymnasts also might find it useful to listen to upbeat music on a Walkman if they need to energize. Again, you can experiment with songs that help you get "psyched."

If you want some examples of how to use anxiety reducers and energy increasers in the gym on each event, see Section III, the apparatus chapters (10–17).

Reducing anxiety and psyching up when you need more energy are some of the most important mental skills in gymnastics. Another very important skill for gymnasts is mental imagery. Imagery allows you to practice any time and any place. The next chapter will help you learn to incorporate imagery into your mental training plan.

6

USING MENTAL IMAGERY TO PICTURE IDEAL PERFORMANCES

Close your eyes and imagine yourself walking into the gym and looking at the equipment. Now imagine yourself getting on the beam and warming up with simple elements (walking across the beam on the ball of your foot, running across, doing a few leaps). Or if you are a male gymnast, do a few warm-up moves on the parallel bars. Stop reading for sixty seconds, close your eyes, and imagine this warm-up.

Did you picture this in your mind? If so, good job! You are using imagery. Mental imagery is a very useful tool in gymnastics. Some gymnasts believe you have to see it in your mind before you can get your body to do it.

According to sport psychology researchers Dan Gould and Nicole Damarjian (1996), the following guidelines will help make imagery effective:

1. Use all your senses. See in vivid color, hear the sounds in the gym, smell the smells in the gym, and feel the equipment as you touch it or how your body feels as it works.

2. Develop control of your imagery skills and visualize positive outcomes. You will want to master control of your imagery skills. Some gymnasts have difficulty visualizing a perfect landing or always see themselves over- or under-rotating a tumbling pass or vault. Don't picture missed landings or falls; instead, nail every trick. Work toward visualizing exactly what you want to perform every time.

3. Use internal and external imagery. Some gymnasts like to watch themselves in their minds as if they were watching a videotape. This is called *external imagery*. Others like to visualize as if they were looking out of their eyes. This is called *internal imagery*. Some gymnasts use a combination of internal and external imagery. Both types of imagery can be effective, and you have to determine which works best for you. You might even find both to be effective.

4. Practice imagery regularly. As we emphasize throughout this book, "practice makes permanent." If you want imagery to work for you, you must make it part of your practice routine so that it is as natural every day as warm-ups. Using imagery consistently will allow it to work for you. We'll give you some tips for how to use imagery in your practices in a moment.

5. Practice imagery in a relaxed state. Research shows that imagery practiced in combination with a relaxed state is more effective than imagery alone. Relaxation can clear your mind of distractions so that you can concentrate on your imagery skills. In addition, when you are first learning imagery skills (just as when you learn anything new), it helps to be relaxed and focused.

6. Develop coping strategies through imagery. Although we mentioned above that you want to visualize positive outcomes, sometimes it helps to visualize an unexpected event

and then determine how you will cope with it. This way, you are prepared for it if it happens and can more easily cope because you have a plan. For instance, you might envision your floor music stopping 3/4 of the way through your routine. You might cope in imagery by finishing the routine without missing a beat. Or you might envision preparing to begin your beam routine and then being delayed because the judges are conferencing about the previous competitor's score. You might mentally practice going back to the waiting area and refocusing as you would if there was still another competitor before you.

7. Use cues or triggers to help your imagery rehearsal. Some athletes find certain words or phrases serve as cues or triggers that help them focus on imagery strategies. For instance, on vault, a cue might be "power" or "push." You can experiment with words that make your imagery more powerful.

8. Practice kinesthetic imagery. To make your imagery most useful, you want to practice actually feeling the sensations in your body as you perform on each event. Feel your muscles, feel your hands sweat, feel your movement in the air. Sometimes on pommel horse, you might see a gymnast close his eyes and slightly move his shoulders as he mentally practices his routine. You might even actually see intentional movements to emphasize a feeling for a skill. For instance, before a twisting tumbling pass, some gymnasts might stand at the corner of the mat, close their eyes, and quickly raise their arms above their head with a twisting motion. In this way, they practice what they will feel as they tumble.

9. Image in "real time." Sometimes it is tempting to image in slow motion to really understand how you do a skill. Sometimes you might be rushed and whip through your imagery very fast. Because you can't actually do your routines in slow or fast motion, it is most useful to visualize at the pace you actually perform. Again, this makes your imagery more like the real thing.

10. Use imagery logs. Whenever you learn new skills, you can best monitor your progress by having a written record. So determine how you will use imagery and keep tabs on what you do, how much you do, and when you do it. This way you can look back and see your progress. You might set it up like Chart 1.

Chart 1: Imagery Log

Date	Time	Describe Imagery	Practice Time	Success
4/28	1:30 p.m.	Practiced 10 double flyaway dismounts off bars with perfect landings; used internal & kinesthetic imagery	5 minutes	A little trouble feeling landings; stuck 3 in workout
4/30	9:00 p.m.	Practiced 3 beam routines in prep for meet tomorrow	10 minutes	Able to image layout pass with solid landings!

Try Exercises 6-1, 6-2, 6-3, and 6-4 to help you develop your imagery skills.

6-1: VIVID IMAGERY

Close your eyes and take a few deep breaths. Picture yourself walking into the gym when no one is there. Look at the layout of the equipment. Notice the colors of the mats and other equipment. Listen to the sounds in the gym, such as the buzz of the lights, the "squish" of the mats as you walk across them, your own breathing. Take a deep breath and notice the smell of the metal on the equipment, plastic on the mats, or chalk in the chalk bins. Touch the bars and feel how your hands grip them. Then put your hand on the beam and feel the leather beneath your fingers. Step onto the floor exercise area and feel the slight spring as you walk on the floor. Now open your eyes.

How vivid were the images you created? If you need to make them more vivid, try imagining in color, hearing sounds, and smelling the chalk and mats.

6-2: CONTROLLING YOUR IMAGERY

Close your eyes and take a few deep breaths. Imagine yourself doing a simple move such as a cartwheel. Stand with your arms raised. Shift your weight to your first leg; place your first hand on the floor. Allow your legs to begin moving over your body. Place your second hand. Feel your straight legs and pointed toes. Bring your legs down on the other side and hands up. Make sure your cartwheel is exactly as you want it to be. Open your eyes.

How easily could you imagine the cartwheel?

As you master control over the imagery of easier moves, you can progress to visualizing more difficult moves with control.

6-3: DOING A ROUTINE WITH IMAGERY

Pick an event. Close your eyes. Breath deeply as you begin to relax. Do a routine mentally in real time. You can do this by timing your imagery and confining it to the real length of a routine. Be sure to use the guidelines that have been discussed for enhancing imagery. Open your eyes. You can try this example with all other events too.

How easily could you perform the imagery? How successful were you in the routine?

6-4: PRACTICING IMAGERY IN THE GYM

Next time you are on beam, mentally rehearse how you want your most difficult tumbling pass to feel before you get up and actually do it. If your coach gives you a correction, imagine doing the skill with the correction before you actually do it again. If you make a mistake, stop. Imagine doing the tumbling pass the right way. You don't want to remember the mistakes; you want to focus on doing the skill correctly. You can use these "in the gym" imagery exercises for all other events too.

Now you have some ideas about how to create images of your ultimate performances in your mind. In addition to imagery, you can use the words you say to yourself to create desired performances. The next chapter will help you use the powers of positive thinking to achieve your goals.

Chainey Umphrey, UCLA gymnast

POSITIVE THINKING: MAKING YOUR MIND WORK FOR YOU

You've probably heard people say, "Think positively!" when someone is faced with a challenge or uncertainty. In fact, your coaches or parents may even say it to you about gymnastics. It's worth listening to them!

What you think about yourself has a huge effect on your performance. A positive attitude toward practice and competition is a must, whereas a negative attitude will only pull you down. Many research studies show that successful athletes have more positive thoughts about themselves and competition than less successful athletes have. Many gymnasts view themselves positively and can perform well. Others struggle with negative thoughts about themselves that result in disappointing performances.

Try Exercises 7-1 and 7-2 to understand how you use positive or negative thinking.

7-1: CONFIDENT PERFORMANCE

Think of a time when you felt positively about yourself and your gymnastics. What was going on in your life and gymnastics at that time? What made you feel positively?

Now rate yourself on the following statements:

How confident did you feel?

Not at all		Somewhat		Very much
1	2	3	4	5

How did you perform in workouts?

Not well at all		Somewhat well		Very well
1	2	3	4	5

How did you perform in meets (if during season)?

Not well at all		Somewhat well		Very well
1	2	3	4	5

How was your general mood and sense of well-being?

Poor		OK		Very good
1	2	3	4	5

At what level was your stress/anxiety?

High		Moderate		Low
1	2	3	4	5

7-2: UNCERTAIN PERFORMANCE

Now think of a time when you felt negatively about yourself and your gymnastics. What was going on at that time in your life? What contributed to your negative thinking?

Now rate yourself on the following statements:

How confident did you feel?

Not at all		Somewhat		Very much
1	2	3	4	5

How did you perform in workouts?

Not well at all		Somewhat well		Very well
1	2	3	4	5

How did you perform in meets (if during season)?

Not well at all		Somewhat well		Very well
1	2	3	4	5

How was your general mood and sense of well-being?

Poor		OK		Very good
1	2	3	4	5

At what level was your stress/anxiety?

High		Moderate		Low
1	2	3	4	5

Now compare your ratings on Exercises 7-1 and 7-2. What differences do you see?

Karen Cogan says this about her attitude:

> I remember how my attitude prior to competition would affect my performance. In some instances, I had tremendous confidence when entering a competition. The warm-up went well, I was hitting everything, and I felt relaxed yet energetic. Of course, when I competed I was nervous, but I could harness the energy into a good performance. Prior to other competitions, I felt a sense of dread and unease. I had a bad feeling that I would fall off beam. In general, I just felt off. I knew I had to lose this feeling but did not know how. Sure enough, I would fall or perform poorly.

All gymnasts experience good and bad practice and competition days. Often how you perform is influenced by your attitude. It is easy to allow a bad performance on one skill or event to drag you down for the rest of the workout or meet. A more helpful approach is to let go of the mistake and focus on what you need to accomplish next. It is also easy to become frustrated when you miss an easy skill or can't stick a landing. You can allow that frustration to affect the rest of your performance, or you can let it go. Attitude has a huge impact on performance. Keeping positive and shaking off errors can make your day. Being negative can lead to an unproductive and frustrating day.

Using self-talk to your advantage. Sometimes in workout you might find yourself thinking things like "I know I can do this" or "I'm not sure of myself on this skill." Sometimes it seems as if you have a voice inside your head coaching you. We call this self-talk. According to Jean Williams and Thad Leffingwell (1996), self-talk occurs whenever you think, whether silently to yourself or out loud, with words. Like having a positive attitude, research shows that successful athletes use more positive self-talk than do less successful athletes. Try Exercise 7-3:

7-3: POSITIVES AND NEGATIVES

- On a piece of paper, write down the positive things you say about yourself and your gymnastics.

- On a separate piece of paper, write down the negative things you say about yourself and your gymnastics.

- Now look at the statements. Do you tend to say more positive things, more negative things, or is there about the same number in each list?

Look at the positive statements you wrote down. Continue saying them and use them in gymnastics. You are off to a good start, and these will be of great benefit to you.

Now let's look at the negative statements, and talk about modifying them. We also talked about thought stopping and replacing in chapter 5 on relaxation. These strategies are useful for maintaining a positive attitude too.

Thought stopping. Remember that when you find yourself saying negative things to yourself, the first step is to firmly say, "STOP!" Next, start working on thought replacement.

Thought replacement. Thought replacement doesn't mean saying unrealistic or untrue things to yourself. If, for instance, everyone in your family is 5 feet 8 inches or under and your goal is to be 6 feet 2 inches tall, it is unlikely that you will even hit 6 feet. Even thinking, "I will be 6 feet tall" will not change your genetics. Likewise, you aren't going to further your gymnastics career if you are still working on a single layout tumbling pass on floor and decide that by thinking positively, you can throw a double layout on your next pass. It is realistic and healthy to say, "I'm not ready for a double layout yet." Replacing that thought isn't very useful.

Look at the skills you can do and have done. When you find yourself in a downward spiral, it is easy to start saying things like "I'll never learn that gainer layout on beam" or "I am such a loser." These negative thoughts are unrealistic (compared to the realistic statements in the above paragraph). So stop right there, and start replacing those negative thoughts with something more productive. Instead, try something like "I know I can get the gainer if I keep working and stay focused" or "I know I am good at gymnastics!" When you are ready to compete a Gienger on bars for the first time, thoughts such as "I'm ready" and "I can do it" are more productive than "I'm probably going to miss."

Countering. Sometimes fears or uncertainty are realistic reactions to gymnastics, but too much focus there takes your mind away from focusing on what you need to do to be successful. So you must learn to counter your fears. For instance, you might think, "I'm afraid of my double back on floor." You can counter by saying, "It's natural to be afraid, but I have done it many times. With good focus now, I can land it solidly." Or you might think, "Everyone else looks so good." Because it is not productive to focus on what others are doing when you need to focus on your own performance, you can counter with "Sure others are good, but I'm good too, and I can show what I have learned. Now let's focus on that."

Reframing. Another useful mental skill is reframing. Reframing involves changing the meaning of a situation or event by changing your perspective (usually from negative to positive). For example, you might have fallen on an event, or you didn't qualify for Nationals. You are allowed to be disappointed when you have worked hard and not reached a goal, but after a while, feeling disappointed doesn't really help you. So it is time to stop feeling disappointed and reframe your experience. With a fall, you might change your focus to the positive with something like "Yes, I fell, but I nailed the other three events and made some significant improvements." If you didn't qualify for Nationals, use it as a learning experience. You might say, "Nationals was really important, but there is next year. I realize that I did not train my new bar routine long enough. Next year I won't make changes so close to Nationals. I will focus on perfecting what I have." Or you might say, "I learned that I wasn't focused enough and allowed distractions to get to me. I know now I must work on focusing for next year."

Shannon Miller discussed how she reframed a disappointing performance:

> Worlds '93, I fell three times in beam finals. I was very disappointed but I was also ill at the time so I wasn't mentally or physically as ready as I should have been. I learned that I can learn from every mistake I make, and each time I become a better gymnast and a stronger person. Looking back, I am glad I made that mistake because I learned that even after a catastrophe like that I wasn't willing to give up. I came back strong in the next event, and later in my career I can look back and say to myself, "Yes, I fell three times in one beam routine at Worlds, but more importantly I went on to redeem myself in the next event, winning a gold on floor." I hadn't given up.

7-4: REPLACING NEGATIVE WITH POSITIVE

Take a few of your negative statements from Exercise 7-2 above. Write them on the left side of the column. Now replace them with more positive ones on the right side. Remember to use the strategies we have discussed in this chapter.

Negative Statements	Positive Statements

You're doing great! You've got it! You'll stick the landing! All these positive statements will become very familiar to you as you practice them in your mental training. And here's one more: You can learn to focus. Read the next chapter to find out how.

8

DEVELOPING FOCUS: HONING YOUR CONCENTRATION SKILLS

Success in gymnastics requires the ability to concentrate, which involves focusing your attention on the task at hand and ignoring any distractions. Oddly enough, you can't force concentration. Usually the harder you try to concentrate, the more frustrated you become. If you try too hard to concentrate, you only think about *trying* to concentrate. To concentrate, you need to relax and feel confident. Then you need to learn to block out distractions and become absorbed in what you are doing. Sometimes you can do this by practicing with distractions. In major events, there may be hundreds of spectators (your parents and friends included) and judges observing you. It can be very distracting to even the most experienced gymnasts. Thus, you must learn to block out the noises and activity and stay focused on your performance.

How do you develop focus and concentration? Here is another instance where practice makes permanent. If you are one of those individuals who naturally can tune out distractions, then you have an advantage in developing concentration abilities. For instance, Karen Cogan remembers dismounting off beam in one meet only to realize that there was a commotion going on in another part of the gym. During Karen's routine, a competitor on bars had taken a spectacular fall, and the crowd had let out a series of "oooohs" while coaches rushed over to see if she was all right. Fortunately, the other gymnast was able to get up and finish her routine. Karen had been so focused on her routine that she was completely unaware of all the activity in the rest of the gym and had finished her beam routine without missing a step.

Different events and meet situations require different types of attention. Bob Nideffer (1986), sport psychologist and author, views attention as having two dimensions, width and direction. Attentional width can be broad or narrow. A broad attentional focus involves being sensitive to many things that are going on around you. A narrow attentional focus involves focusing directly in front of you and, in a sense, knocking out your peripheral vision. Attentional direction can be internal or external. An internal attentional focus involves focusing on your own feelings or thoughts. An external attentional focus involves focusing outwardly to other things and people around you.

Taken together these dimensions form four combinations:

1. Broad-External: Involves assessing the situation and cues in your environment. For example, when you are warming up on floor for a meet, many athletes are tumbling at the same time. You have to have a broad external attentional focus to make sure you don't mistakenly tumble into another gymnast.

2. Broad-Internal: Involves analyzing game plans and strategies. In gymnastics you might determine how best to use your free warm-up before timed warm-ups begin in a competition. You could decide what events you need a little

extra preparation on and plan to have a few extra minutes to warm up there.

3. Narrow-External: Involves focusing on external cues while blocking distractions. For instance, on the beam, you want to focus only on the beam, not on the surrounding environment. You want to ignore what is happening on other events or in the crowd.

4. Narrow-Internal: Involves focusing within yourself. For instance, when you practice mentally rehearsing routines, you are using a narrow-internal perspective.

A skilled gymnast is able to shift on demand among these different attentional styles.

Most gymnasts cannot shift attentional focus this easily, and therefore can benefit from practicing concentration skills. If you would like to shift more quickly, you will want to start with some basics. Try these exercises.

8-1: LEARNING TO FOCUS

1. Take some time and focus on your breathing. See how long you can be aware of your inhales/exhales and the movement of your chest without allowing your mind to wander.

2. Then pay attention to the sounds you hear around you. Notice any voices or noises in your environment. Really focus on these.

3. Next, focus on how your body feels. Feel your arms, head, neck, shoulders, stomach, and legs. Notice the feeling of the chair you are sitting in or the pressure of the floor you are standing on.

4. Now attend to your emotions and thoughts. Again, see how long you can maintain focus without your mind wandering.

5. Now choose an object in your environment and look at it. Focus on this object. Now, shift your focus to what is happening around you. Shift back to the object. Can you easily shift your focus?

After you can do these exercises reasonably well, you can begin practicing similar exercises as you train. Go into the gym and

practice steps 1 through 4 there. Then use the gymnastics apparatus as the object in your environment to practice step 5.

Eventually incorporate these exercises into your training
routines. For example, during warm-ups, as you are running
around the floor mat to get your blood flowing, focus on your
breathing only. Concentrate on the sound and rhythm of your
breathing and the feel of your chest as it rises and falls. When
you do a beam routine, focus your eyes only on the four inches
in front of you. Don't take your eyes away (with the exception
of doing any aerial moves). See how well you can minimize the
distractions in the gym.

Cue words. Athletes also find that using attentional cue words
can increase their ability to concentrate. A cue word is a word
you choose that reminds you of something, in this case, to
focus. You might want to pick one portion of a performance on
which you really need to concentrate to be successful and find
a word that triggers focus for you. For instance, on vaulting,
you may need to focus on pushing off the horse well. So your
cue word as you are preparing to run down the runway might
be "push." Your cue words can be even more general. For instance, if you find your mind wandering on your beam routine,
your cue to bring you back might be "focus" or "stay tight."
You will have to experiment with cues that help you maintain
a general focus or concentrate on a specific element.

The following are some examples of cue words that gymnasts can use:

General cue words:	Vault:	Bars:	Beam:	Floor:
• focus	• go	• swing	• tight	• smile
• calm	• push	• catch	• steady	• breathe
• relax	• fast	• cast	• land	• punch
• tight	• explode	• up	• straight	• twist
• ok	• run		• hold	• leap
• do it	• stick			• power
• go for it now				• explode
				• pull

8-2: TUNING OUT DISTRACTIONS

Next time you are in the gym and there is a lot of activity that doesn't involve you (floor music blaring, coaches shouting hints on how to improve to other gymnasts, teammates shouting encouragement to each other), try the following exercises.

1. Close your eyes and clear your mind. Now do some mental subtraction. Start with 100 and subtract backwards by 7s.

2. Close your eyes, and do a gymnastics routine mentally.

3. When you are done with these exercises, ask yourself (a) how easily could I focus on subtracting numbers or the routine, and (b) how easily could I tune out distractions?

If you could tune out distractions, then you have developed some good focusing skills that will serve you well in gymnastics. If you had difficulty tuning out distractions, then practice. Remember, practice makes permanent. Find other occasions when there is a lot of activity or make audiotapes of noise or conversation. Then practice mental math or imagine routines. Don't expect to be perfect the first time around (or even the first few times) at something you haven't practiced much. After practice, the distractions will likely have less influence on your ability to concentrate.

Competition simulation. You can practice concentrating under pressure and with distractions by simulating competition situations (where you create a meet-like environment and pretend you are actually competing). This strategy allows you to practice as you compete and is used by many successful gymnasts. Competition simulation is discussed in more detail in chapter 18.

It's not hard to see how useful focusing skills can be for gymnastics. The ability to concentrate will set your performances apart from those of gymnasts who are more distractible. It's also good to focus on the future and what you want to achieve. This is a different type of focus with different strategies. The next chapter discusses goal setting as one effective way of achieving your dreams.

Peter Vidmar at UCLA

GOAL SETTING FOR SUCCESS

How do you get where you want to be in gymnastics? Setting goals is a powerful strategy for reaching your dreams. Goals help you stay focused and give you steps to take in achieving your ambitions. Research shows that goal setting is effective in enhancing athletic performance. To get the most out of goal setting, keep the following guidelines in mind. These guidelines have been suggested by Bob Weinberg (1996), a sport psychology consultant and researcher.

1. Set both short-term and long-term goals. Short-term goals are the stepping-stones to larger, long-term goals. It is overwhelming to think about performing an entire bar routine without major errors when you have barely mastered the individual elements. So decide what you want to ultimately accomplish, and then break it down into manageable parts. Keep your ultimate goals in mind, but also have daily and weekly goals to focus on. For instance, if you want to learn a front flip on the beam you might go through the following goal "ladder."

   a. Learn front flip on floor.

   b. Do front flip on line on floor.

c. Do front flip on low beam with spot.

d. Do front flip on low beam without spot.

e. Do front flip on high beam with mats stacked underneath.

f. Take away stacked mats, and do front flip on high beam with spot.

g. Do front flip on high beam without spot.

You can use similar steps to learn other skills as well.

2. Make goals specific and measurable. Often gymnasts will set vague goals such "I want to do my best." Although wanting to do your best is a common goal, it is not very specific. Goal setting is more effective if you choose specific and measurable goals. For instance, if you are working on beam dismounts, your goal might be "to stick seven of ten dismounts" rather than "do some good dismounts."

Here are some other vague goals. See if you can make them more specific.

Vague	Specific
Do the best I can	_____
Improve my endurance	_____
Get stronger.	_____
Increase the difficulty in my routines.	_____
Work hard.	_____

3. Set realistic, yet challenging goals for your level of ability. Set goals that you have a good chance of achieving, but don't make them so easy that you face no challenge. If you are a beginner, don't expect to learn a double twisting double back first off! Set a goal of learning a single back tuck. If you are advanced, setting a goal of learning a layout will be too easy. Find something that pushes your skills just a bit further than they are presently.

4. Set deadlines. Your goals should have deadlines. Don't just tell yourself that you want to become a Level 7. Write down when you want to accomplish that goal. This will help you stay focused in your training because you know the deadline is coming up, so keep working!

5. Set your goals in positive terms. Decide what you will do, not what you won't do. So don't say, "My goal is not to fall off beam," but instead say, "I will hit this beam routine."

6. Write down your goals. It has been said that "a goal not written is only a wish." You are more likely to accomplish your goals if you write them down and review them regularly. Writing them down allows you to refer back to them and adjust them as needed. Committing goals to paper also helps maintain your focus as you work toward them.

7. Set performance goals. It is very important to set goals based on your own level of performance rather than the outcome of winning or losing. Although it is hard to ignore final placements in gymnastics meets, if you focus on winning, you may not focus enough on what you need to do to win. You are looking too far ahead to the future outcome of the competition and will forget to focus on hitting the routine you are doing now. So, set goals for your performance without comparisons to others. If you reach your personal performance goals, that is something to be proud of right there! Placing or getting awards will go along with top performances.

8. Get support for your goals. It is much easier to reach goals if you receive encouragement from others. Your parents, coaches, and teammates might play a useful role here. If you face obstacles, these important other people in your life may be able to help you overcome those obstacles. In fact, many members of the women's 1996 Olympic team mentioned that they couldn't have been successful without their parents.

9. Evaluate your goals. Goals do not need to be set in stone to be effective. In fact, they are not useful if they turn out to be too difficult or too easy. You need to periodically evaluate

your goals and your progress toward them. You might do this with your coach or on your own. This allows you an opportunity to adjust your goals as needed or add new ones.

Using the guidelines discussed above, do Exercise 9-1.

9-1: GOAL SETTING

1. One of my long-term goals is _____

2. Some of the short term-goals I must achieve to reach that long-term goal are
   a. _____
   b. _____
   c. _____
   d. _____

3. Things that will assist me in reaching these goals are
   a. _____
   b. _____
   c. _____

4. People I will ask to help me are
   a. _____
   b. _____
   c. _____

5. Obstacles I might face in reaching these goals are
   a. _____
   b. _____
   c. _____

6. To overcome these obstacles, I will
   a. _____
   b. _____
   c. _____

Now you have learned basic mental skills that will make a positive difference in your gymnastics performances. You can apply these skills to any event as needed. The next several chapters give you specific ideas on how to use these skills for each event.

THE APPARATUS

In this section, each of the gymnastics events for women and men is discussed. Physical skills for each event are first briefly outlined, and then useful mental skills for that event become the main focus of the chapter. Keep in mind that most of the challenges mentioned for a particular event could be faced on any event. Likewise, the corresponding mental skills suggested to meet those challenges can be used for all events as needed. To avoid repetition throughout the book, however, each challenge is generally mentioned under only one event. For instance, dealing with fear is discussed on bars and beam, but you might find that you actually feel fear the most on floor. So think about the strategies suggested for beam and bars, and alter them to fit your needs on floor.

In addition, the chapters on vault and floor apply to both men and women because these events are so similar for both genders. The other events, however, are relevant for either men or women and are treated separately. In addition, the women's events are examined in depth, but issues for the men's events are summarized because much of the discussion on the women's events also applies to men's events. So men will want to read the chapters on women's events to understand how to apply sport psychology strategies to their training.

The most important thing to remember as you read about each event is to practice, practice, practice your mental skills! For mental skills to be effective, you must incorporate them into your training routines and make them become habit. You must immerse yourself in your mental training as you do your physical training, and then you will see results.

VAULT (MEN AND WOMEN): VAULTING TO SUCCESS USING MENTAL STRATEGIES

The physical skills. Vault requires speed, power, and timing. Even though you are not judged on your run as you approach the horse, this is where your vault starts. The faster you go as you sprint down the runway, the better your chances of producing a spectacular vault. Your takeoff on the board as well as angles of contact with the horse must be good. This positioning allows you to get maximum height and distance on your vault and gives you enough air time to do as many flips and twists as you need. Body position and landings are extremely important in this event.

The mental skills. Mentally, vault can be challenging in many ways. Vault is the only event that is not a routine. Rather, it is a single element that is over in a matter of seconds. Because your entire score depends on this one element, vault sometimes has an all-or-nothing feel to it, although the good news is that women get two tries. If you have a poor takeoff or slightly miss one hand on the horse, your entire vault and score are affected. You have little room to make up points. So you need to be completely focused as you vault. On the other hand, many competitors enjoy vault because you just do it without much time to let your thinking get in the way of your performance.

Imagery. Vault lends itself well to the use of mental imagery. The following is an example of how you can use imagery to take yourself through a vault. You can use imagery on vault to build your confidence the night before, ten minutes before, or one minute before you compete. You also can use this type of exercise to rehearse your vault for practice or to overcome fear. In this script, the vault is a handspring front being performed in a competition situation. Remember, this is only a sample, and you will need to alter it to fit your own personal needs, but this gives you an idea of how you can take yourself through an imagery exercise.

Script: You are standing at the side of the vault runway, and you are next up to compete. Take a few energizing breaths, and move your arms and legs to get the blood flowing. Step up to your starting point on the vault runway. Look ahead and focus on the horse down the way. As you start running, feel your leg muscles working. They are powerful as they propel you down the runway, but at the same time the movement seems effortless. You feel your speed increase as you near the springboard. You take your last step on the runway and hit the board at the perfect point that gives you the most spring. You swing your arms to meet the horse. Your feet leave the board and move upwards. Your back has a slight arch as you push off the horse with immense power. You feel yourself going up as you tuck and complete the one and one half rotations. You are aware of your position in the air and can feel a perfect landing coming. You open up, your feet hit the mat, your knees bend, and you stick your vault. You straighten your legs and stand lifting your arms up and emphasizing your perfect landing. Then you turn, full of confidence, and salute the judges.

Managing anxiety. Some gymnasts experience anxiety related to vault. They wonder if they will get their steps right, wonder if they can get high enough and rotate enough to flip and twist and land on their feet, and wonder if they will stick their landing. The energy generated by anxiety can actually be used to your advantage. Because vault requires power and speed, you can put that anxious energy into your run and push off the vault. Some gymnasts like to reframe their anxiety and want to feel activated before vault because they need that energy to run fast down the runway.

Energizing. Vault also lends itself well to energizing techniques. If a gymnast does not feel "psyched up" enough or feels fatigued before competition or workout, then energizing techniques can be useful.

Remember that before deciding to adopt energizing strategies, you need to assess whether you need them. If you are the type of gymnast who always has a tremendous amount of energy or feels anxious, then you may not need energizing techniques. For you, energizing may make you more anxious or cause you to over-rotate your vault. If you need a little extra zip, see chapter 5 for tips on using energized breathing, energizing imagery, cue words, and music to give you an edge.

Challenges Specific to Vault

Gymnasts can encounter a number of specific problems on vault, but these problems don't have to take you out of the competition. You just need to know how to handle them. Here are some pointers from a mental perspective.

Balking during competition. Sometimes your steps are off, or you can't get adequate speed during your run, or you feel as if you won't hit the board in the right place. So you stop or run past the board. We call this *balking*. Every gymnast has done this at one time or another in practice without much concern, but it can be especially disconcerting during competition. It is easy to think that you missed your steps once, so you will do it again. Balking can be a major psych-out, but only if you allow it to affect you. First, forget about it. If you balked, it's okay. Take a few deep breaths, refocus yourself, and check your starting point again on your way back to the beginning of the runway. This might mean that you run back as if you were going to vault to check your mark. Remember that you have vaulted hundreds of times before and have found your steps. Also, while running back to the start, you have another chance to warm your muscles up so you should be able to really fly down the runway next time. Don't focus on the possibility of using up your energy (or getting tired) from that extra run. Your adrenaline will kick in. Now let go of the first run, and focus on what you know how to do. This careful preparation will help you get it right the next time.

If you are concerned about balking, you can use coping imagery to prepare yourself for the possibility of doing so in a meet. Take a moment to visualize yourself in a meet situation on vault. Imagine you have just balked on your first vault. Imagine how you feel. You would probably be flustered and nervous. In your imagination, see and feel yourself take some deep, calming breaths. Say to yourself, "I can do this." Forget the first vault, and focus on the cues that help you vault well. Prepare for the second vault and see yourself coming through with lots of confidence to nail the vault that counts. In this way, imagery can help you be prepared for and solve potential problems before they happen.

Falling on your first vault (women). If you fall or somehow make a major error (for instance, you didn't do the vault you meant to do) on your first vault, you may feel pressure to perform on the second vault. You may see it as your last chance. If it is an important competition, the pressure is even greater. Think about Kerri Strug's second Olympic vault—that was pressure. You do not have to let the pressure prevent you from performing your best. You merely have to rethink and reframe the situation. Here is an opportunity to prove to yourself that you can do this vault, and you can come through when it counts. If you typically land your vaults well and this first one was a fluke, think of it as just that, a fluke. Now just do the vault the way you know how. Go back to your starting point, visualize and feel yourself vault in perfect form. Energize yourself and go. If your vaulting has been inconsistent, focus on what you need to do to vault well, visualize a perfect performance, energize, and go. Don't waste time thinking about what you might do wrong or what bad luck that was on the first vault. Focus your energy on what you need to do and what you can do right.

Sticking the landing. On any event, but especially with vault, a perfect landing is important. Precious tenths can be lost when extra steps are taken. One way to focus on sticking your landings is to use goal setting. (Remember, you can use goal setting to perfect landings on other events too.) Try Exercise 10-1 with vault.

10-1: LONG-TERM AND SHORT-TERM GOALS

Choose a long-term goal and then list short-term goals that will help you reach that goal. Include a time frame for reaching each goal.

Example:

Long-term goal: Stick 8 out of 10 vaults consistently in practice by competition season.

Short-term goals: (Reach one every 2 weeks.):

1. Stand on the horse, jump onto the landing mat, and stick the landing.
2. Become comfortable with just doing the vault, without concern about landings.
3. Stick one vault per workout.
4. Stick 2 vaults out of 10.
5. Stick 4 vaults out of 10.
6. Stick 6 vaults out of 10.
7. Stick 8 vaults out of 10.

Now use this format to set your own personal goals.

Long-term goal:

To be reached by (date) _____

Short term-goals and time frame for each (to help you reach your long-term goal):

1. _____
2. _____
3. _____
4. _____
5. _____

FLOOR EXERCISE (MEN AND WOMEN): TUMBLING TO THE TOP

Physical skills. Floor exercise requires both power and grace. Gymnasts must demonstrate multiple tumbling skills that include flips and twists, moving forward and backward. Floor is probably the most physically demanding event, and therefore, you must learn to pace yourself well. Floor requires endurance to get through three tumbling passes and the dance or transitions in between. Also, you want to tumble as high during the last pass as you did during the first to leave a good final impression with the judges. Women must be able to dance and leap in between tumbling passes, playing to the music and crowd. Men perform tumbling, leaps, and strength moves as transitions in their routines.

Mental skills. Often gymnasts experience less anxiety about competing on floor than in other events because it is impossible to fall off floor (although you can fall on this event!). Even so, floor requires mental focus and activation control for gymnasts to perform their best. Women must mentally switch from powerful tumbling to the relatively more restful and graceful dance portions, all with flow and continuity. More so than the others, this event allows a gymnast to play to the judges and crowd. In the words of Kerri Strug, "It takes enthusiasm, positive energy, and positive attitude" to excel on floor. If a gymnast looks as if she is enjoying herself out there, she is likely to get the crowd behind her as they marvel over her interpretation of the music. This type of "performance" requires confidence and the ability to switch focus from dance and tumbling to the crowd and judges.

Men also must shift from powerful tumbling to controlled, precise balance and strength moves. Although men do not compete to music or have the same opportunity to play to the crowd, they can still use personality and flair to get the crowd behind them.

Energizing strategies. Activation levels usually need to be more on the energized side. Energizing strategies can be used for floor much the same way they are used for vault. In particular, energizing is useful for tumbling passes and toward the end of the routine. You can use energized breathing, energized imagery, or upbeat music. (See chapter 5 for more detail on each of these.)

Notice how Tori uses energizing strategies in the following case example:

Tori was so tired. In fact, she had fallen asleep in the car as her mother drove her to the gym. As they pulled to the door, she awakened, feeling as if it was all she could do to get out of the car. She knew her first event would be floor today, and she did not see how she could muster the energy to make it through the four required routines. She remembered, though, that music could get her psyched up.

As she walked into the gym, she put a tape into her Walkman and began listening. As she listened, she imagined her body as a powerful machine. She could feel all the muscles working in sync together and getting stronger and stronger. She took some deep breaths and began pushing the fatigue away. Gradually, she increased her energy level. She visualized herself performing her tumbling passes: round-off, backhandspring, double back, perfect landing. As the song ended and she got ready for warm-up, she noticed that her energy had returned, and she no longer felt like going back to sleep. In fact, she had a good feeling about this workout, and the four floor routines no longer seemed like an impossible task.

11-1: ENERGIZING IMAGERY

Try some energizing imagery. Close your eyes and begin to focus on your breathing. With each inhale think "energy in" and with each exhale think "fatigue out." Visualize your muscles becoming active and powerful. As Tori did, view your arms and legs as powerful machines or springs. Visualize your first tumbling pass and perform it with energy and power.

Confidence builders. Floor is an exciting event to watch. It is even more exciting if the gymnast adds dramatic flair to her performance. In short, she must have enough confidence to go out there, look the judges or audience in the eye, and put on a show, whether it is slow and dramatic or fast and upbeat. Although men might not be as dramatic as women on floor, men still have the opportunity to show off their strength and balance moves. This type of attitude demonstrates confidence. In fact, many gymnasts are able to draw energy from a crowd when spectators show their appreciation for a routine or applaud. This energy can add to the fun and excitement of a performance.

It is understandable that when you first begin training, you may have to focus so much on remembering your routine or doing new tricks that you cannot concentrate on adding your personality to the routine. You may find you can only have a more narrow focus. Once you have more practice, however, you will find more opportunities to focus on your presentation as well as to focus on projecting an air of confidence. You can learn to occasionally shift to a broad focus to include the crowd, and since gymnastics scores are based partly on artistic impression, how you present yourself can affect your score.

Sometimes it is difficult to walk out on the floor with your head up and a smile on your face when all you can think about is throwing that double full (or double back or full-in) on your first tumbling pass for the first time in competition, but one of the tricks to being confident is acting confident. If you start acting confident (whether you feel it or not), you can actually begin to convince yourself (and other people) that you are confident. You've probably seen gymnasts walk out onto the floor for warm-ups looking relaxed and sure of themselves. They get on each event, throw all their skills as if they know what they are doing. Sometimes we call that "winning the warm-up." The confident image that they show can help them feel more confident throughout the meet itself. Even if you don't feel confident, experiment with acting confident. You might be surprised to find that it helps.

Acting confident does not mean going overboard and acting cocky or criticizing other gymnasts. Confidence is an inner state that you develop for yourself separate from any other gymnast. So show your confidence, and at the same time respect your competitors.

Positive self-talk. Confidence also can be built by using positive self-talk. Positive self-talk is discussed in more detail in chapter 7. You can walk onto the mat like Tracy with your head down saying, "There's no way I'll make this double full (or double back or full-in); I know I'll come up short." Or you can keep your head up and walk tall like Gina saying, "This is a new pass for me, but all I have to do is go for it with all I've got. I've done it before, and with some adrenaline, I can nail it." Who would you expect to be more successful—Tracy or Gina? If you talk like Gina, you would have a much better chance of landing your new tumbling pass.

Focus. Floor requires the ability to shift focus quickly. You must be able to go from narrow/internal (being aware of body position) to narrow/external (looking at the corner of the mat

Kim Hamilton, UCLA gymnast

where you will do your next tumbling pass) to broad/external (playing to the crowd). You need to rapidly switch back and forth throughout the routine. You also need to practice switching focus quickly in practice so that it comes naturally during competition. Set aside one practice per week where you deliberately practice switching your focus on attention from your technique to your presentation.

12

UNEVEN PARALLEL BARS: GETTING INTO THE SWING OF THINGS

Physical skills. The uneven parallel bars require swing, timing, and endurance. A gymnast's routine must be in constant motion as she swings from bar to bar, changes directions, and performs release moves. A gymnast must learn to trust that she can let go of the bar, do a move (often several feet in the air), and be able to grasp the bar again. There are a lot of diverse skills to be mastered for one event.

Mental skills. On bars a gymnast needs a moderate amount of physical and mental energy to maintain her swing. She must learn to focus and concentrate to do a variety of moves in the right position to regrasp the bar. She needs to manage possible fear as she flies high in the air between and above the bars.

Imagery. As with vault, imagery can be very useful in mastering bars. You can practice imagery on one element that is new or is giving you trouble, or you can practice a whole routine. For instance, if you are trying to learn a giant, you might practice Exercise 12-1.

12-1: USING IMAGERY

You jump and grasp the high bar and pull yourself up into position on the high bar. You take a moment to prepare, take a deep breath, and cast to a handstand. You hit the handstand perfectly and allow your body to swing down. You can feel a good grip on the bar and your body swinging effortlessly with speed. You hit the bottom and tap as you swing up the other side. You can feel your body lifting, and you shift your grip. Your body comes over the top of the bar, and you are ready to do another giant with power and swing.

Once you master imagery of single elements, you can visualize your whole routine. You can do it any time; the more the better. You can do it before workout, before a bar routine, after the routine to correct errors, and after workout. Make sure you image positive outcomes and feel yourself in full control in your imagery.

Managing fear on bars. Gymnasts often become fearful on bars because of the height required for release moves. In addition, some of these moves are blind, and athletes must trust their air sense and position to clear the bar and regrasp it. Chapter 23 offers some general strategies for dealing with fear that can be applied to bars.

Let's also take an example specific to bars. Elizabeth was learning a Gienger. She had become comfortable with flipping above the high bar and had learned how to fall when she missed the high bar. On one try, however, she almost had it but at the last minute peeled off the bar and slid under the low bar on her back. When she stood up, she was dazed and scared because this fall was more frightening than usual. She became concerned about attempting her Gienger again for fear of a repeat performance.

One way of overcoming such a fear is to use a psychological technique called *systematic desensitization*. With systematic desensitization, you create a hierarchy (a list in order from least to most fear-provoking) of potentially fearful events. Then you visualize each event in order starting with the least fearful. As soon as you can visualize that event without experiencing anxiety, you move to the next event on your hierarchy. If you feel anxiety while visualizing an event, you use relaxation skills to manage the anxiety and return to the one before it on the hierarchy (which produces no anxiety). From there you work your way back up to that next event. Elizabeth might produce a hierarchy such as the following:

1. Kip on high bar.

2. Giant swings.

3. Gienger in the pit.

4. Gienger with stacked mats in the pit.

5. Gienger with stacked mats (not in pit) and coach spotting.

6. Gienger with coach spotting.

7. Gienger with coach standing near.

Elizabeth might begin visualizing #1 (kip) and likely would feel little if any anxiety. Then she could work her way up to visualizing a #7 (Gienger with coach standing near) without anxiety. It might take her several tries before she felt comfortable even visualizing her Gienger again, but by gradually working her way up to the last event on her hierarchy, she can learn to manage her anxiety.

Challenges Specific to Bars

Sore hands. You can't do gymnastics without running into sore hands from bars. Sore hands and rips can keep you from doing the amount of training you want or need on bars. Prevention is the best medicine when it comes to your hands. It is important to develop a consistent plan for maintaining the health of your hands and to be extremely dedicated to that plan. Even if you take all the care you can, though, you will not avoid soreness and rips completely. Of course, it seems that it is always right before that major competition that you rip . . . badly.

First, keep in mind that some injuries (including blisters and rips on hands) are severe and require special care or sitting out of practice or competition. Always consult with your coach and/or physician when you have any type of injury. We would never advocate practicing when you have a severe injury and could do more permanent damage. The pain you feel is your body sending you a message to take it easy, and it is important to listen. When the rip is a minor inconvenience, you can use the power of your mind to focus on gymnastics.

How can you deal with the pain? Let's see what Jaime and Kelly did. During Jaime's last workout before Regionals, she got a major rip that was bleeding and painful. "Great," she thought. "That's all I need." She thought about her hand all the next day and worried about how it would affect her bar performance. When she got to warm-ups for the meet, she felt the pain as soon as she touched the bar. She warmed up as little as possible on bars and waited for her turn. Instead of focusing on her routine and her strengths, all she thought about was how much her hand was going to hurt. When she did her routine, she missed elements that she never missed in competition. When she got off the bars, she realized that her hand had not been that painful, but she was so worried about it that she did not perform near to her potential.

Kelly had a similar rip on her hand from her workout before Regionals, but she took a different approach. Yes, the rip was an inconvenience, but Regionals were just too important to let something like a rip keep her from reaching her goals. She cared for her hand over the next day and did as much visualization of her bar routine as she could. She knew that if she mentally practiced, she could make up for not having as much chance to physically practice. She got to the meet and went through a brief warm-up, focusing on making every element count and doing the most efficient bar warm-up she could. She visualized her routine two more times. Just before her turn to compete, she was so focused on what she needed to do to hit her bar routine that she forgot about her hand. She attacked bars and hit one of her best routines of the season.

Notice how differently Jaime and Kelly handled the inconvenience of getting a rip before Regionals. You, too, can choose to focus your mind on gymnastics rather than your hands.

Let's take a real-life example of success in spite of a rip. During the 1996 Atlanta Olympics, Jair Lynch had a horrible rip in the thirty-second warm-up before the parallel bar finals. His routine required a lot of swinging, which would be a strong irritant to the rip, but he knew this was the most important performance of his career and was able to block out the pain and focus on what he needed to do. He won the silver medal!

You might handle sore hands or rips differently in workout than you do in competition. Let's start with workout. First, you need to determine how severe the damage to your hands is. Will it be more useful for you to keep working with the hope your hands will heal by the next workout, or do you need to give them a rest for now? If you choose to continue, it is tempting to focus on the pain at the expense of your elements or routines. If you shift the focus from gymnastics, though, you will not get your full value out of practice. Then you are working with pain for only limited gain. So keep your mind on your routines. If your attention begins to wander to your hands, recognize what has happened and shift it back to what you are doing. If the pain becomes too severe and distracting, then you must make a decision about whether or not to end your bar workout.

It is hard for a gymnast to sit out of competition because of sore hands or a rip, and most do their best to compete anyway. Much of the time, you can count on your adrenaline to kick in, and the pain becomes less noticeable. So if you decide from the start not to worry about your hands and not to focus on the pain (because you probably won't notice it much when you are up on bars anyway) you have an advantage. Remember, anything that takes your focus away from your gymnastics will keep you from performing your best. So make a decision to forget the hands and do what you know how to do. Once you get on the bars, focus on your routine. Like Kelly, use mental imagery to practice and prepare before the meet.

Keep in mind that bars is not the only event in which minor pain gets in the way of an optimal performance. You can slightly twist your ankle or pull a muscle on any event. As long as training with some pain will not cause further or permanent damage, the above strategies can be used on the other events as well.

BALANCE BEAM: WALKING A STEADY LINE WHILE STAYING FOCUSED AND RELAXED

Physical skills. Beam requires precision, steadiness, and fear-lessness. It requires a gymnast who can tumble, leap, and dance in a straight line on a piece of leather-covered wood that is approximately four feet off the ground and about four inches wide. She has to demonstrate anxiety control, flexibility, grace, and power all at the same time. Beam probably requires the most diverse skills of all the women's events.

The mental side. Beam is often seen as the most difficult event. Just staying on the beam sometimes becomes a primary goal. It is easy to slip and fall and even easier to have a major wobble. Anxiety can have a tremendous effect on a gymnast's performance. Inability to control anxiety can be a gymnast's downfall on this event more than on the other events. In addition, fear is a major factor and can increase the anxiety. It is not surprising with all the aerial (and sometimes blind) moves that fear of injury can hamper a gymnast's beam progress and performance.

Anxiety management. From a psychological perspective, the ability to manage anxiety is probably the key to being a great beam worker. Many gymnasts can learn spectacular moves on the beam and can do them in workouts, but will wobble or fall, or both, during a meet because of the anxiety. In fact, gymnasts often make errors during competition on moves they

Karen Cogan at UCLA

never miss in workout because of the added anxiety. Learning the relaxation skills discussed in chapter 5 will give you an edge on beam. First, you will need to identify when you feel anxious and what makes you feel anxious. Try Exercise 13-1:

13-1: MANAGING ANXIETY

Think about when you feel anxious about beam. Look at the examples below and put a check mark under "usually," "sometimes," or "rarely" as that statement applies to you.

	Usually	Sometimes	Rarely
• before you even get to the gym	___	___	___
• just prior to beam workout	___	___	___
• during beam workout	___	___	___
• only for new skills	___	___	___
• before competition	___	___	___
• during meet warm-ups	___	___	___
• a few minutes before you compete	___	___	___
• during competition	___	___	___
• some other time (list) _____	___	___	___

Look at your check marks. Are there only some times when you feel anxious? Or do you feel anxious most of the time? Assess the times you feel most anxious so you can target those times as you begin learning anxiety-control strategies.

Now think about what specifically makes you anxious, and check the appropriate column.

	Usually	Sometimes	Rarely
• learning new beam skills	___	___	___
• a particular beam skill	___	___	___
• a skill on which you have been hurt before	___	___	___
• the need to be perfect	___	___	___
• frustration with your performance	___	___	___
• fear of a coach getting angry	___	___	___
• something else (list) _____	___	___	___

Now look at what most often makes you anxious. Focus here as you begin learning new relaxation skills.

Once you identify when you become anxious and what makes you anxious, then begin using relaxation skills (discussed in chapter 5) as part of your practice. Use these skills any time you start to feel some anxiety. With enough practice, relaxation will become second nature and can be used during a meet when anxiety levels are even higher.

Focus strategies. Another important psychological skill for beam is the ability to focus. Shannon Miller, 1996 Olympic Gold Medalist on Beam, offers her insights on what it takes to mentally excel on beam:

> It takes a great deal of focus to do balance beam. You must learn to focus on all of your body parts, making sure they are in the right place. You also cannot be afraid; you have to go all out on every skill. You must be able to block out everything that is going on around you.

Likewise, Jaycie Phelps emphasizes the importance of focus:

> Your focusing ability is the most important quality for beam. I always focus my mind at four inches and nothing else. You have to be able to block out noise and all surrounding movements [so that you have] tunnel vision.

Imagery. You can also positively affect your beam performance by using mental imagery to practice for competition. Karen Cogan recalled her use of imagery:

> I remember lying in bed at night visualizing my beam routine perfectly from start to finish several times before dropping off the sleep. I could feel my body going through the motions and landing each element without a wobble. I know I performed better because of this extra practice.

With practice, you will find that visualizing your routines on beam can give you that extra advantage.

Challenges Specific to Beam

Going from low beam to high beam with a new skill. So you've perfected that flip-flop layout on the low beam and can do it fairly consistently now. The next step is to take it to high beam. It should be no problem, your coach reminds you. One beam is the same as any other, right? WRONG! Every gymnast has experienced "low-beam confidence" only to feel that she is starting over once she steps up on high beam to do the exact same move. The only difference is a meager four feet in the air (and a new mental perspective, of course). On one hand, it is clear that the skill you have been doing easily on low beam is the same one you should be able to do on high beam. If you go for it as you did on the low beam, you will be successful. You will need to continue to remind yourself that you have mastered it and can make the transition to high beam. On the other hand, it is hard to forget that the stakes have literally been raised. Injuries are more likely with that added four feet. Often you can transfer skills (especially easier skills) from low to high beam without much difficulty. In other cases, you can use a spot, stacked mats, a medium-level high beam, or any combination of these aids, before working your way up to a regulation-height beam (without mats!). Once you gain your confidence at each of these progressions, you can more easily transfer the confidence to the next level of difficulty.

Before going any further, let's add a few words about safety. When you are practicing a new skill on the low beam, you are bound to have some misses. So when you try it on high beam, you are also going to miss some of the time. You will want to make sure that any misses on the low beam are "safe misses" so that you do not risk injury on the high beam. A safe miss might involve getting your hands or feet, or both, on the beam but being slightly crooked in the air and then falling. Missing your hands and feet completely would not be considered a safe miss. When (a) you are hitting the majority of the time on low beam, (b) any misses are safe, (c) and your coach agrees that you are ready, then you can move to high beam.

How do you cope when you've mastered a move on low beam, gotten spots or stacked mats on high beam, and still cannot get yourself to throw the skill? Sometimes you need to start over. Go back to low beam and prove to yourself (again) that you can easily do the skill. Then work your way back up to the high beam. Sometimes you can get another spot to remind yourself that your body really does know how to do the trick. It might take a little longer and involve some back tracking, but persistence pays off. Setting small goals to reach the ultimate goal of doing the skill on high beam will help here. If you stick with it and maintain a positive attitude, you can master that move on the high beam too.

Sometimes it helps to shift your focus. Often when you won't go for a skill, it is because you are thinking about it too much or too many "what ifs" are running through your mind. What if I miss my foot? What if I get lost in the air? It is important to shift your focus in these instances to something more productive. Focus on how it feels to throw the skill on the low beam. In fact, you might want to focus on something completely unrelated to gymnastics. Remember, your body knows what to do; just let it work without allowing your mind to get in the way. You also can use imagery to perform the skill successfully in your mind.

Competition order. Another part of the mental side of beam is when you compete on it in a meet. Many gymnasts do not want to draw beam as the final rotation in a meet. The thinking is something like . . . "If I have already made errors during the meet, then I might have to count on a high score on beam. There is always the chance I will fall, and come to think of it, my routines haven't been all that consistent lately. And now that I'm thinking even more about it, I'm getting really nervous, and I'm just sure I'll fall."

This type of negative psych-out thinking is counterproductive. You beat yourself with these types of thoughts. You need to turn your thinking around. Use the self-talk skills from chapter 7 in this situation. So you have beam for your last rotation. The order of your events should not distract you from focusing completely on your next event. Competitions have been won by a good performance on beam during the last rotation. Focus on the hard work you have done on beam and how ready you are. Use imagery to practice your routines and relaxation strategies to keep your anxiety in check. You can do well on beam during the first rotation or during the last rotation. It might seem corny, but convince yourself that you like (no, love) beam. You need to work with beam, not against it, so give yourself every advantage.

A fall early in your routine. On any event, but especially on beam, it is easy for a gymnast to psych herself out if she falls on her mount or some early element or tumbling pass. If your goal is to hit a routine, then you may be disappointed at missing that goal so early on. Gymnasts often find themselves giving up and having a number of additional falls, even on elements that are usually consistent for them. Much of the trouble lies in a gymnast's thinking. First, you need to start with good thinking habits in practice. Remember that practice makes permanent. Turn your thinking and attitude around entirely in workouts. Complete every routine you begin, even in training. This is good practice in case you have an early fall off beam in competition. You want to fight for every skill and every routine in practice as if it were in competition. Never give up.

Then continue to use this mind-set in competition. If you fall or have a major deduction early in your routine, there is nothing you can do about it. It has happened. But you still have most of your routine left, and you can still leave a good impression. You might have lost 3/10 or 5/10, but you can still get an acceptable score. Don't lose another 5/10 or more by giving up. You still have the chance to end on a good note and leave a positive impression.

Shannon Miller provides a compelling example of why gymnasts should focus on every skill and routine even if there are previous mistakes.

At Championships in '96, I fell on beam (my first event). I came off the beam disappointed and about ready to give up. (I had been through a lot to get there with a wrist injury.) Instead of yelling or telling me it was over [my coach] looked straight at me and said, "Well, it's time to get going." He said, "You have some new skills on all three of the other events, you had fun learning them, now let's go out there and show them off." After that I knew I just had to go out and give it my best shot. I hit all three of the other events and ended up winning the meet. But what I remember most is that [coach] Steve [Nunno] didn't give up on me even when I had almost given up on myself.

Often in gymnastics, the best performers are those who learn to refocus after a mistake, not those who worry about being mistake-free.

POMMEL HORSE: CIRCLING WITH MENTAL SKILLS

Physical skills. Pommel horse is completely different from all the other men's events. The other events involve swing and backwards-and-forwards motions. Pommel horse involves circles instead. Gymnasts often have more difficulty catching on to the necessary skills for circles. At some point, though, it finally clicks. All you can do is two circles for a while, and then suddenly you are doing five. Then it becomes fun, but, most important, you must be patient and keep working on circles until they become second nature.

Mental skills. Like women's balance beam, pommel horse is often considered the most difficult event for men, especially in competition. For this event, the gymnast must stay calm and not get too psyched up. He must be able to focus and block out distractions.

Staying calm. Too much activation will make your routine feel out of control, and then you are more likely to fall. This is a problem especially in competition. A few deep breaths before a routine can you help relax in competition. See chapter 5 on managing anxiety and chapter 13 on beam for specific relaxation skills.

Focusing. As with beam for women, this event for men requires the ability to focus. An external-narrow attentional focus is helpful here. You will want to attend to the pommel horse equipment (external) to know where each end of the horse is and where the pommels are as you move through your routine. At the same time, you will want to narrow your focus so that you won't be distracted by what is happening in other parts of the gym or arena. Also, it is often helpful to focus on only the first one or two skills of your routine as you approach the horse to perform. Usually if those skills go well, you are off to a smooth start and can stay more relaxed and focused for the rest of the performance. If you look too far ahead into the performance, you may not be thinking about what you need to do NOW. That's when you are more likely to make errors.

Imagery. Visualizing routines is especially helpful on this event. You often see gymnasts stand to the side of pommel horse before competing and mentally prepare themselves. Sometimes you see them actually move their bodies as they visualize their routines. Kinesthetic imagery is useful on this event when you are learning circles or preparing a routine for competition. Try the imagery examples outlined in chapter 6 on imagery and chapter 12 on bars, but use circles or scissors as the focus of your image.

Handling a fall. Falls are always disappointing. Sometimes it is tempting to get right back up to continue the routine. If you fall, don't jump right back up. Instead, take some time to refocus. Stop, gather your senses, take some breaths, and continue. You still have the rest of the routine to perform, and this strategy could save precious tenths. As with any event, you can still get a respectable score even with a fall.

Peter Vidmar shares one of his Olympic experiences on pommel horse. You'll see how he had to manage his activation, use focus, and practice imagery.

Going into the (1984) Olympic pommel horse finals, I was tied for first place with Li Ning of China. He went first and scored a perfect 10.00. Now I'm good at math, and it didn't take me long to figure that I had to be perfect for the Gold. That meant that the first time my knee bent, I would lose the Gold. I knew everything needed to be perfect. I needed to get off to a good start. I put a lot of energy into the first part of the performance. I tried so hard in the beginning, that I felt fatigued earlier than I wanted to. Then I felt fear, that I had gone out too hard. So I had this debate in my mind (which happened in a matter of seconds). Do I do my hard dismount and risk breaking form or an easier one? I decided that the judges would know if I did the easy one. So I made the decision [to do the hard dismount], and that gave me a surge of adrenaline and the energy to finish the routine with the hard dismount. I was able to handle the pressure [of the Olympic finals] because I was ready for it and had trained for it. I always trained to do the perfect routine. I had the imagery of that routine.

Scott Keswick, UCLA gymnast

15

RINGS: DEVELOPING YOUR (MENTAL) STRENGTH

Physical skills. Rings requires power, strength, and swing. Because boys will not develop strength until later in adolescence, they need to focus on their swing at first. In addition, the handstand position is very important in this event, so perfecting the handstand is a good place to start. Once a boy develops his strength, he can begin focusing more on this event.

Mental skills. Because rings involves so much strength, adrenaline in competition can be a gymnast's best friend. The main mental skill involves harnessing the adrenaline so that it works to your advantage.

Monitoring your energy level. You want to be energized and excited for this event to bring on the adrenaline. Be confident that the adrenaline will come as you prepare to compete, and then it is a question of how to handle this energy. You can use the nervous energy to your advantage, so that you feel much stronger throughout the routine, especially at the end when your strength might otherwise be fading. At the same time, you need to keep the energy in check so you are not tempted to use it up in the middle of your routine. For instance, you might think "I've got adrenaline to spare. I can hold that cross for an extra second." But if you do that throughout your routine, you will run out of energy at the end. It is best to compete what you train (e.g., hold your strength moves only as long as you do in practice). The adrenaline can be used to make the end of your routine shine.

Energizing strategies. If you are having difficulty finding enough adrenaline in a workout or as you prepare for competition, you can use energizing strategies. See chapter 5 for ideas on how to energize and review chapter 10 on vault. Also, if you can't get enough energy for a competition, then you need to examine how important this competition is for you. Sometimes when you are unmotivated, it is harder to find the energy.

PARALLEL BARS: USING WHAT'S BETWEEN YOUR EARS BETWEEN THE BARS

Physical skills. Parallel bar routines consist of swing, flight, and strength elements. This event now requires more dynamic multiple flipping skills (such as a giant double back in between the bars catching in an upper arm support) than were required ten years ago. In fact, some newer moves have even been adapted from high bar.

Mental skills. Parallel bars is much like pommel horse in that you must control your energy, especially in competition. In addition, the more dynamic moves require intense concentration because there is more room for error.

Activation control. As with any event, you must find your optimum degree of activation. Too much activation will cause you to lose control, and you must become a master at managing your energy levels. See chapter 5 for suggestions on reducing activation if you need that. Also the chapters on beam (chapter 13) and pommel horse (chapter 14) are useful for parallel bars.

Focus. Because of the newer release moves, parallel bars now involves more risk. Coming down correctly is extremely important to avoid injury. You will notice that many of the competitors now wear arm pads to protect them from the impact as they hit the bars. Therefore, maintaining your focus is extremely important. One momentary lapse in your concentration can mean a miss, fall, or even injury.

Cue words can be useful on parallel bars where your focus has to shift from swinging and flipping to balance and precision and back to powerful movements again. Gymnasts can practice moving from cue words such as "go," "push," and "now" to "steady," "tight," and "stick" as they master the transitions in their routines. Staying mentally focused and being able to shift focus will aid gymnasts in staying physically healthy.

We've already discussed in chapter 12 how Jair Lynch coped with a severe rip on parallel bars during the 1996 Olympic finals and earned a silver medal. His performance is a wonderful example of how the ability to focus can pay off. It's enough of a challenge to focus during the Olympic Games with all the spectators and pressures, but Jair also was concerned about a painful rip. On top of that, Jair had missed a medal four years earlier in Barcelona by only a hop on his dismount. So to medal in Atlanta, he had to be completely focused on every part of his routine, down to a stuck dismount (which he did!). He was able to focus on his performance, making it as near perfect as possible, and ignore the distractions of a painful hand. See chapter 8 for ideas on learning focusing skills and chapter 13 (beam) on using imagery for maintaining focus and perfecting routines.

Tim Daggett, UCLA gymnast and Olympic Gold Medalist

17

HIGH BAR: GETTING INTO THE SWING OF THINGS II

Physical skills. High bar is one of the most spectacular events for men. Swing is important, with giants being the basic element. In addition, men are required to do a number of release moves, sometimes twelve feet above the ground.

Mental skills. Often the biggest obstacle to overcome on high bar is fear. Good breathing, self-talk, and imagery are very helpful in overcoming anxieties on high bar. In addition, focus is important on high bar. You can't just go through the motions as you might on some other events because lapses in concentration can lead to more serious falls.

Anxiety management. High anxiety can be a hindrance on this event. When anxious, you focus more on the anxiety and less on the difficult moves you are doing. Finding an optimum activation level (not too little and not too much) will be beneficial to your performance. Breathing is a useful way to control anxiety. A quick moment to take a few deep breaths before performing a skill that causes anxiety can be useful. See chapter 5 on managing activation levels for details on using breathing and other suggestions. Also, chapter 12 presents an example for using systematic desensitization to overcome fear after a fall on a Gienger on uneven parallel bars. The same systematic desensitization can be used for Giengers on men's high bar.

Positive self-talk also can be useful in reducing anxiety on high bar. It is easy to talk yourself into errors, falling, or not going for a skill with negative thinking. For instance, if you are working on a Gaylord flip, you might prevent yourself from learning it by saying things like "I'll never get high enough to complete the flip and catch the bar" or "I'll probably hit the bar and hurt myself." This type of negative thinking only increases the chances of missing the skill or injuring yourself. Instead, focus on what you can do. Say, "I have practiced with a spotting belt and I know how to do it," or "I'll be okay if I go for it hard without holding back." See chapter 7 on positive thinking for other ideas on improving self-talk and chapter 23 for more on overcoming fears on this event. The imagery techniques discussed throughout the book also are useful here.

Focus. Because high bar is a risky event, you must constantly focus on what you are doing to hit. If you miss and begin to fall, you must quickly shift your focus to Plan B. Plan B involves knowing how to fall correctly so you avoid injury. Mentally preparing by using coping imagery (practicing a mistake and coping with it) can be useful for potential high bar falls. See chapter 8 to learn focus strategies.

Mental preparation can help you transfer your good practice routine into competition. Tim Daggett scored a perfect 10.00 in the 1984 Olympics on high bar. Here is how he describes his preparation for the routine and the routine itself.

[It was the] '84 Olympic Team Finals. I was fifth up, Peter [Vidmar] was next. We knew we could win. It was the most petrifying experience but the most invigorating. There was a lot of walking-around space in Pauley Pavilion. I was pacing as each person went, we were coming closer to our lifelong fantasy. It got worse and worse. I focused on each guy.

I looked into Scott Johnson's eyes, and I saw he wants it. I looked into Mitch's [Gaylord] eyes, and I felt like I spent so long preparing myself. It was overwhelming. I walked up the steps thinking I couldn't walk up the steps, couldn't lift my arms. I was chalking up and had no idea what to do. I saluted the judges. The second I touched the bar I knew there was no way I would fall. I felt electricity go through my body. I had two releases, and I came around to look for the bar and knew the bar would be there. I don't know why it was that way. As I grabbed the bar I knew I had done it a million times and prepared for thirteen years. I had a positive shift. I trained pretending [workouts] were the Olympics. That was one preparation that gave me confidence. The past helped me know I could do it.

18

SIMULATING COMPETITION

Why do some gymnasts work hard in the gym and do near flaw-less routines, but "choke" under pressure? Why does she per-form a simple move (like a split leap on beam) easily in workout but surprisingly fall when in a meet? Why does he easily do a scale in a floor routine in the gym but stumble in a meet?

Most gymnasts understand the difference between practice and competition. After reading this book, you can easily see why the pressure of competition can wreak havoc on a gym-nast's performance. We've been saying, "Practice makes per-manent" throughout the book, but how do you practice the feelings that go along with competition without actually being in one? The answer is to simulate competition. In other words, create a practice environment that is as similar as possible to a meet. You can use a variety of the psychological skills we have discussed so far to accomplish this.

"Talk" yourself into a meet in practice. Pretending you are in an important competition can create a meet environment. You can intentionally set up a hypothetical meet situation, with the expected distractions and procedures that you would find in a real meet. For instance, when Peter and Tim Daggett trained for the 1984 Olympic Games, they simulated meet situations. They worked hard the entire workout, focusing on what they had to do to train optimally. Then they reached their last event, which usually was high bar. Having exerted so much effort throughout the workout, they were understandably tired, but working hard when you are tired is when it counts. So they would say to each other, "Okay, this is the Olympics. We are neck and neck with the Chinese (the favored team at the time) going into our last event. Whoever wins this event will win the Olympic Team Finals. We have to hit!" Each took turns being the announcer's voice as the other prepared to "compete." Hitting that routine became a very important goal. They were elated if they hit and beyond disappointment if they missed.

Then an interesting thing happened. In the actual 1984 Olympics, they really were neck and neck with the Chinese, and high bar really was the last, deciding event. And they did hit their routines, clinching the team gold for the United States. Setting the stage during training with a hypothetical situation and creating an environment that was similar to the Olympic Games allowed them to feel more comfortable when they faced the pressure of the real thing. That type of situation was familiar to them, and they could focus on hitting strong routines rather than coping with an unexpected, pressure-filled situation.

There are a variety of other ways you can simulate meet situations. Some of these:

- Asking everyone in the gym to stop and watch as you perform a routine.

- Having someone videotape your routine or take photographs as you do a routine. This strategy is especially useful if you expect to be competing in front of cameras.

- Asking your coaches or teammates to "judge" you. They can act as judges, adding up deductions and giving you a final score.

- Having an intersquad meet with real judges, scores, and awards.

Hold a dress rehearsal. Related to meet simulation is the dress rehearsal. Generally a gymnast's workout attire is different from her competition leotard. That's a good thing because you want to save that leotard for special occasions! If you train in tights or short-sleeved leotards, you might not be used to the feel of long sleeves or bare legs when you dress for a meet. In addition, just putting on your competition leotard often creates a different atmosphere and sense of competition readiness. Some gymnasts might feel good because they look good; others might feel nervous because they associate this leotard with competition. There is just something about putting on a competition uniform that can change how you perform. Rather than waiting for that feeling during meets only, you will want to practice with it. That's why a dress rehearsal can be useful during training. You may want to use this strategy sparingly so that you really get a "meet effect" each time.

Warm up as in competition. Related to a dress rehearsal is a warm-up rehearsal. Warm-ups in a meet are usually different from the ones you do in the gym. So to prepare yourself for what you will really experience, you can conduct warm-ups in the gym as if practice were a meet. For example, take twenty minutes (or some predetermined amount of time) on each event to do a full warm-up; then do one routine on each event. Make sure to take a one-touch warm-up before each routine.

Practice going first or last. Where you compete in the competition lineup is usually by the luck of the draw. You could go immediately after warm-ups, or you may need to wait, sometimes for a long time. Don't wait until you get to the meet to practice for these situations. Make them happen in the gym, where you have the opportunity to practice coping with any lineup position. So do your warm-ups as in #3, and then go first; or do your warm-ups, and then wait. Watch your teammates for a while, and then practice getting into the state of mind you need to be focused.

Use mental rehearsal. Because your options for competition simulations and dress rehearsals might be limited, you can rely on mental rehearsal as well. You won't have to create an elaborate setup or arrange for judges to come to your gym if you use your mind. You can mentally create competition environments and practice your routines any time and any place. Check chapter 4 for tips on using mental imagery. You will want to create a realistic and vivid picture in your mind of what the meet will be like, including any distractions or possible challenges. Then visualize yourself performing your routines perfectly in that situation. The more you do this, the more comfortable you can become in competitions.

Prepare for the unexpected. What do you do if your music stops in the middle of your floor routine? How do you cover if you happen to cast a little too hard on that first handstand on bars and go over the top? How do you cope if the audience is really noisy just before your beam mount? Don't wait for a meet to decide how to handle each of these situations. Practice coping with these unexpected events in the gym so that in a meet a solution comes naturally. Consult with your coach, and make a plan. For instance, if your floor music stops 3/4 of the way through your routine, you may choose to finish the routine without music and without missing a beat. If you cast too far on your handstand on bars, have an "alternate" routine that you can do to cover. If the crowd is noisy before your beam routine, remember your focusing strategies and center yourself with a cue word. You can use imagery to practice being in the situation and then responding appropriately.

The suggestions listed above are only some of the ways you can prepare for a meet. You can experiment with these and then add others that will help you with the challenges you expect to face. Remember that practice and preparation will make the high pressure of competition more manageable.

Now you have some ideas on how to apply the general mental skills described in section II to the specific apparatus, but that's not all there is to the mental side of gymnastics. Your relationships with the other important people involved in your training can influence your psychological well-being. The next few chapters explore the effects of those relationships, starting with parents.

Co-head coach Scott Bull, UCLA, spotting former Bruin Denise Scott

RELATIONSHIPS WITH OTHER PEOPLE IN GYMNASTICS

A gymnast does not train and compete in a vacuum. There are many important people, especially coaches and parents, who contribute to an athlete's success. Some of these people can add pressure and stress to a gymnast's life as well. This section addresses the roles of these important people in gymnastics. These chapters help gymnasts learn how to draw on the support of these individuals and also provide guidelines for how these individuals can best influence a gymnast's success.

PARENTS

Parents are vitally important to the well-being of their young athletes. Without parental support and assistance (both financial and emotional), it would be difficult, if not impossible, to succeed as a gymnast. Most parents want what is best for their children in school, sport, friends, relationships, and life; and many parents can find ways to provide the best for their children. But because parents can have such a strong influence, they sometimes exert unnecessary pressure on young athletes. This pressure can make the sport less enjoyable for young gymnasts. This chapter examines both positive and negative parental involvement. It is useful for parents and gymnasts to read as it includes ideas for enhancing parent-child relationships.

Positive parental involvement. Let's start on the positive side of parental involvement in sport activities. It is important to emphasize that parents do so many things right and are often instrumental in the success of their child. Some of the gymnasts from the women's 1996 Olympic gold medal team told us the following in responding to the question "What did your parents do right?"

> Amanda Borden: "Everything! They were my parents—there to support, love, care, cheer, ease the pain, and most importantly they loved me no matter what. I couldn't have done it without them."

Jaycie Phelps: "They stayed out of the gym. And they supported every decision I made. They never pushed me to do anything. They are a big part of my success."

Kerri Strug: "[They] supported me through the rough times but knew the fine line between getting involved and staying away."

Shannon Miller: "My parents supported me all the way. They also made sure that I had balance in my life. And they made sure that no matter what, I knew they loved me, as their daughter, not only as a gymnast."

There is so much good that can come out of a family's sharing involvement in their child(ren)'s gymnastics. When parents are interested in and supportive of the young gymnast's progress, everyone benefits. Parents can share in the triumphs and accomplishments and help cope with the disappointments. It is natural for parents to want to share in the winning moments and congratulate their child after a stunning performance, but parents also can be there just as strongly for the mistakes and frustrations. Parents of gymnasts can show great compassion. Karen Cogan remembers one gymnast who was devastated after several falls off beam during one meet. She headed over to the stands, and her mother simply held and hugged her while the daughter cried. That was the best thing the mother could have done.

Parents can become highly involved in their child's training and know as much about the terminology and judging as the athletes do. Anyone else listening to a conversation between parent and child about workout that day might think they were talking a foreign language, but parents and gymnasts can build their relationship with this shared interest and support.

Gymnastics also can become a family affair, especially during the competition season as everyone packs up to spend the weekend (or a good part of it) at a meet. Gymnastics parents build relationships with each other just as the gymnasts do. It is like having an extended family when all the parents and gymnasts from a given team (and maybe other teams as well) are supporting all the team members. The camaraderie that is developed can be very rewarding. Soon, the parents as well as gymnasts are sharing a social network, and these relationships can last a lifetime. Karen Cogan's mother still remains good friends with another gymnastics mother she met more than twenty years ago.

Of course, attending meets can be stressful for the parents as well as the gymnasts. When the parents share their child's goals, the parents may also feel anxiety as they hope for a good performance and their gymnast's safety. Karen remembers her father commenting that "the girls go home with medals, and the parents go home with nervous breakdowns" because of the anxiety he felt in just watching her compete. But going through this type of experience can bring families closer.

Any parent reading this will recognize that "spectator anxiety" can feel similar to "performer anxiety." It should be no surprise that the same types of ideas for controlling "performer anxiety" discussed in chapter 13 will work for "spectator anxiety" as well. Parents, see the box below for some suggestions.

- Deep breathing: When you feel anxiety building, close your eyes and take a few deep breaths.
- Exercise: Although you might not be able to take a five-mile run at a meet, you can get up and walk around the gym or outside to relieve some tension.
- Distract yourself: Find something of interest to occupy your attention. Karen's mother used to keep track of every competitor's scores to manage her anxiety. At Regionals and Nationals that's a lot of scores.
- Talk to other parents or spectators: Because parents develop bonds as they see each other weekend after weekend, they can serve as a support to one another. Talking about anxiety or other unrelated topics can help bring the tension down a notch.
- Progressive Muscle Relaxation and Cue-Controlled Relaxation: Don't think this is reserved only for your child. You can learn the same relaxation response by training your muscles to relax and pairing your own cue word with the relaxed state.

Pressures from parents. Parents can also exert too much pressure if they become overly invested in their child's sport. Sometimes parents can get so absorbed in their goals and desires for their child, that they can't or don't see the child losing interest in the sport. Maybe the parent dreamed of being a good athlete or world-class gymnast but never could achieve that goal. Now here is an opportunity for the child to reach a similar goal, and the parent does not want the child to miss it. The child then feels pressure to perform well and keep training when he or she would rather be doing something else.

Parents can also pressure their child more subtly. There are parents who just want the best for their child. They want the best coaches, the best training, the best college, or the best scholarship. Although the parent is not obviously pressuring the child, the child feels the pressure at some level. The child can be especially troubled if he or she does not share that same need to get all the best in gymnastics that the parents do.

The Olympic champions we interviewed have discussed some of the ways parents can place pressure on young gymnasts:

Shannon Miller: "Some parents lose sight of what is really important. That is, that their kids are happy. Gymnastics is supposed to be fun. Some parents seem to think their kids can't be happy unless they come home with a gold medal. This is not true. The happiness is going into the gym and learning new skills and being with friends."

Amanda Borden: "[Some parents] live through their kids . . . when the parents want it more than the kid. Gymnastics is a sport and it's for fun. A parent should be there to help guide and teach their child, but most important to see them have an enjoyable life."

Parents can become extreme in their involvement with their gymnasts. At one extreme is the parent you see at workouts or at meets, yelling directions or criticisms from the stands or clearly pushing a child. This parent might try to tell the coach how to coach and be a very obvious fixture at all workouts or meets. Take a look at this letter from young gymnast:

Dear Mom,

> There's something I need to tell you, but I'm afraid of what you might say. So I'm writing you a letter.
>
> Gymnastics used to be fun for me. I couldn't wait to get to workout each day. And I was glad you supported me so much. But somewhere along the way everything changed. As I learned more skills and did better in competition, I felt more and more pressure. Now gymnastics is not fun anymore.
>
> One of the reasons is you. I know you want the best for me, but when you yell at me from the viewing area as I am practicing my beam routine, I feel so embarrassed. Everyone looks at you and at me, and I want to crawl into a corner and hide. And during the last meet when I fell on my dismount off bars, I saw you throw up your hands in disgust. Then you lectured me on the way home about how careless I was and how this is a waste of your money. I wanted to die.
>
> I can't go on like this. I don't want to do gymnastics if it isn't fun . . . and it isn't anymore. I hope you can understand why I feel this way.
>
> Sara

On the other extreme is the parent who is rarely involved. Some athletes may want more than anything for their parents to come to their meets and support them. Without support, these gymnasts may feel ignored and neglected. Neither extreme—too much involvement or too little—is helpful to a gymnast. Parents need to be aware of how they treat or influence their young athletes.

For Gymnasts

How Can a Gymnast Deal With Parental Pressures?

Talk to your parent. Sometimes young athletes feel pressure from a parent but have never told the parent how they feel. The first step is to talk about the pressure and how it makes you feel. For instance, you might explain to your father that you get so nervous you can't sleep or you dread workouts because of the pressures. Second, be clear about what you want or need. If you need your mother to give you more space at competitions, tell her (nicely, of course) that you can concentrate much better if she is sitting quietly in the viewing area.

Talk to your coach. If you do not get the results you want by talking to your parent, and you feel comfortable with one of your coaches, see if he or she has some ideas about dealing with parental pressures. The coach might be able to give you some suggestions about how to communicate your needs with your parents. Your coach also might be able to talk with your parents about how to help reduce the pressure you feel.

Talk to your teammates. Although they may not be able to do anything about the pressure you feel, sometimes just talking about it with someone who understands can help you feel better.

For Parents

How Can Parents Learn to Be Supportive Without Becoming Overly Involved?

This is a difficult question to answer because every case is so different. The short answer is that parenting a gymnast is a balancing act—how appropriate for this sport! There is a fine line between supporting and pushing. Here are some things to consider as you examine your involvement:

1. Listen to your child. Often your child will tell you how he or she is feeling about gymnastics. Sometimes the child will

say it clearly; other times, it is not always with words. So you have to pay close attention. If you aren't sure, ask your child direct questions and really listen to what he or she says and doesn't say.

2. If your child does not want to talk about gymnastics (or answer your questions about it), then allow that privacy. Maybe he has had a bad day in the gym where nothing went right. Maybe she had a minor conflict with a teammate or coach. Sometimes gymnasts would rather leave the problems in the gym. However, if you sense that something critical is behind the silence, you must make a decision as a parent about how much to pursue finding an answer. This is where you are walking a fine line, and unfortunately, there are no easy answers.

3. Help your child make good choices about continuing or leaving gymnastics. One of the most difficult decisions for a gymnast to make is when to end his or her involvement in the sport. Often parents have a large role in this decision and can potentially exert pressure. Again, there are no firm answers because every situation is different, but here are a couple of guidelines to consider. A child should probably not be permitted to make a major decision, such as dropping out, after a big disappointment or a conflict with a coach. These issues should be examined first, and then, after some time, a decision about remaining in the sport can be made. On the other hand, if a child appears down over a long period of time, then a decision to stop participating may be more appropriate. Just make sure any decisions about staying or leaving are in the best interest of the child.

It is helpful for parents to be aware of their potential for pressuring their children and to take responsibility for changing behaviors that are stressful. The next chapter offers tips for parents who are raising young gymnasts, including some thoughts on minimizing parental pressures.

PETER VIDMAR'S TIPS FOR PARENTS RAISING YOUNG GYMNASTS

A number of years ago, I was asked by *Parade* magazine to write an article to parents on raising a young athlete. At the time I was fairly new to this thing called parenting with a young son Timothy (named after my close friend Tim Daggett). The only way I thought I could credibly discuss the topic was to use my parents as the model and write about how they treated my gymnastics career. But Timothy is now 14, and he is joined by Christopher, 12, Stephen, 10, Kathryn, 8, and Emily, 5. I am now gaining firsthand experience on dealing with children in sports, and not just gymnastics. There are also Little League and soccer to take up our afternoons and weekends.

However, as I prepared this chapter, I realized that my observations on being a good gymnastics parent have really changed very little, and I thank my mother (who recently passed away) and my father for setting such a good example of how to raise my own children, regardless of whether or not any one of them chooses to pursue gymnastics. So I would like to include many of my comments from that earlier article, with some additions directed specifically toward this sport. Although I certainly can't lay claim to any complete knowledge on this topic, I hope other parents will appreciate my perspective.

On July 31, 1984, in a packed house at UCLA's Pauley Pavilion, I raised my arm to signal the head judge on the horizontal bar. I was the last performer for the U.S. team in the most important competition of my life, the men's Olympic gymnastics finals. Moments earlier, my best friend, Tim Daggett, had completed a stunning 10.00 performance. Now it was my turn. I went through my routine, landed my piked full-twisting double-back dismount and, with a 9.95, removed all doubt as we upset the favored Chinese team for America's first-ever gymnastics team gold medal.

After an emotional ceremony, all six of us were rushed down to a corner of the arena, where we were interviewed by ABC Sports. I wanted to speak to the millions of excited children who were watching television that night. I remember saying, "All I know is that I hope there are a lot of kids out there who run out and join gymnastics clubs."

Indeed, almost overnight, thousands of girls and boys throughout the nation who wanted to be like Mary Lou Retton, Kathy Johnson, Julianne McNamara, Mitch Gaylord, or Bart Conner joined such clubs. Unfortunately, many of them dropped out after only a few weeks when they realized just how rigorous training can be. But many stayed in and paved the way for what we now enjoy in USA gymnastics.

In any sport, the young athletes who make it to the top succeed because of a variety of influences, including coaching, good facilities, and most important, their own drive and determination to achieve excellence. The attitude of parents also is significant. Based on many of my own experiences, I believe there are some important things mothers and fathers can do to have a more positive influence on their young athletes.

Know what to expect. My initial interest in gymnastics came from my father, John Vidmar, who was a gymnast in high school. A bout with polio when he was 29 left one leg somewhat crippled, so he was unable to participate with our family in sports other than swimming, but he and my mother, Doris, supported every activity we participated in, whether it was my brothers' wrestling or my sisters' dancing (I come from a family with six children).

Often parents don't realize what they're getting themselves into when their children take up a sport. I'm sure my parents weren't prepared. I began seriously training at age 11. Aside from the substantial cost of my lessons, my parents made many other sacrifices that involved time and effort. Once-a-week classes soon became six-days-a-week workouts, with my parents driving to the gym and back twice each day. Family meals, if we had them at all, had to be scheduled around my workouts. During my entire career, we went on only a couple of family vacations, and even then, we had to make sure my workout needs were met. For 10 years, my parents were restricted in their ability to move to another home because I had to be close to my gym club and my coaches.

Get involved. Even in the midst of what would seem to be one inconvenience after another, my parents never complained or grew tired of my gymnastics. They were willing to put in whatever I put in. The more time and effort parents contribute to their children's activities, the more they'll reassure their children that they are genuinely interested in what they do. Besides, parents will enjoy it more themselves if they're actively involved in some aspect of their child's sport. When I was just starting to compete, I'd get a kick out of my dad in the stands—a calculator in one hand, some paper in the other, and a pencil in his mouth as he frantically tried to get every score of every gymnast in the competition. I guess that being an engineer, he found that was the best way to handle the pressure (he soon learned to just sit back and enjoy himself).

It's always special when parents take the extra interest. During an important competition when I was 13, I mentioned to a coach in an embarrassed sort of way that I couldn't go to an athlete's party because I had to meet with my parents, who had come all the way to New York to watch me compete. Very firmly he responded, "Don't you ever be embarrassed that your parents like to follow you to competitions. I was a national champion in my sport, and my father never came to see me perform." I quickly learned to be thankful that I could hear my parents' cheers in the stands.

Share in the victories—as well as the disappointments. When young athletes perform poorly in competition or get injured, they can easily become depressed. Here parents must show that unconditional love that is so important in a relationship. Rather than express disappointment, parents should tell their children that they're proud of their children's efforts and have confidence that things will get better. I remember missing a crucial fly ball in a Little League baseball game and getting yelled at by my coach, another player's father. Losing the game was enough punishment for me; his yelling did little for my self-esteem and only put more pressure on me the next time a fly ball was hit toward me.

Injuries are very common in competitive athletics, and they are difficult to cope with. Injured athletes need support from their coaches and teammates, as well as their parents.

Don't push. Although most parents are enthusiastic supporters of their children's athletics, a few can take that enthusiasm too far. I know a young athlete who showed an incredible amount of potential at a very young age. At first, he was excited to train, and he learned skills at an unusually fast rate. Eventually, however, his coach noticed a change in his demeanor and a significant drop in his motivation. When the frustrated coach confronted the 13-year-old, the boy broke down and started to cry. Apparently, he was being pushed too far. Every night after some already-exhausting workouts, his mother would make him exercise, and every morning she would make him run as she followed him in the car. The athletes must own their own goals; their parents can't own the goals for them.

It's important to know the difference between supporting and pushing. This mother's intentions may have been good, but it became her will more than her son's that he be a great athlete. As soon as he was old enough to make his own decisions, he quit.

Timothy, my oldest, loves soccer and baseball and has played in leagues for some time now. We thought it only natural that Christopher would want to follow suit and join his big brother in these sports, and he really expressed an interest. So we enrolled him in soccer, and he joined Timothy's team. After seeing him sit down in the middle of games, watch the ball go right by him with no effort to really go after it, and find great joy in the various insects that crawl in the playing field, game or no game, it became glaringly obvious that soccer is not for Christopher and that he really has no interest in competitive team sports at this point in his life. That's absolutely fine. You should see how much he loves school, piano, and yes, gymnastics. All we did with soccer was insist that he see it through the end of the short season, because quitting halfway through something you start is not a good habit. I doubt he will want to go back to soccer soon, or at all, but if he does, it will be his own choice, and my wife and I will be there for him.

Talk openly about your concerns. It is always important for athletes, coaches, and parents to communicate effectively. Parents should try to understand the coach's philosophy but should tell him or her what they feel is important for their child's overall development (for example, proper emphasis on schoolwork, family commitments, and religion).

Most important, parents should see their role with the proper perspective. As I mentioned, the key to success is the athlete him- or herself. Parents, coaches, and teammates may all want an athlete to reach his or her potential, but that individual must want it him- or herself.

I think it's important to note that when it comes to competitions, we parents need to be careful how we act and react on the sidelines or in the bleachers. It's very disturbing to see a parent loudly berate the judging or actually cheer when an opposing gymnast (someone else's son or daughter) falls or makes a mistake. We all know the most powerful way we teach our children is by example. What lessons do we teach if our own children see us behave this way (that it's okay to celebrate other people's misfortune or setbacks so long as it advances our own position)? I realize that these incidences are rare, but they should never happen.

I thank my parents for their enthusiasm and sensitivity throughout my gymnastics career, especially during the first few years, when it was most difficult for them. At the beginning, there was no way of knowing that their skinny little son with the "chicken legs" would become an Olympic champion; they made the sacrifices simply because they knew I loved gymnastics. As I became more successful, I think my parents became a little concerned over their own enthusiasm. Every once in a while, my father would say to me, "Son, you know how much your mother and I love your gymnastics and how proud we are of your accomplishments. But you're not doing gymnastics for us, are you?" I'd always smile and say, "No, Dad, I really love the sport."

My parents set a good example for me in raising my own children. As I mentioned at the beginning of the chapter, my wife, Donna (a former UCLA gymnast), and I have three sons and two daughters. The boys attend a terrific program with the U.S. Gymnastics Training Center in Laguna Hills, California. I have no idea what level of commitment, if any, they will show in this sport or any other, but I do know that they will have a dad and a mom who will try their best to give them the appropriate support and involvement they need to have a youth full of positive experiences and lasting memories, win or lose.

Parents are not the only adults who will play a significant role in a gymnast's career. Coaches are very central as well. The relationships a young athlete develops with the coaches will likely be one of the keys to success. The next chapter examines those relationships.

21

WORKING WITH YOUR COACHES

Coaches play a vital role in shaping a gymnast, whether it is for beginning local meets, collegiate competitions, or the Olympics. Athletes could not be successful without experienced and devoted coaches. You are probably aware that, in general, a coach's job is to help a gymnast reach his or her maximum potential. Sometimes that involves strongly encouraging or challenging the gymnast to work harder or learn a new skill. At the same time, coaches need to find an appropriate balance between challenging and supporting the athlete.

There are a variety of coaching styles, and you will want to find coaches who work well with your personality. Once you find a coach you like, it is important to establish a good relationship with him or her. Ideally there will be mutual respect between a coach and the gymnast, as well as open communication. Amanda Borden, Jaycie Phelps, and Shannon Miller all discussed their relationships with their coaches and what their coaches did right.

Amanda Borden: "Mary Lee [Tracy] did a lot right. To be successful you have to work together. Our relationship is the key to our success. We were both eager to learn. We communicated with each other, but most importantly we are great friends."

Jaycie Phelps: "She [coach] believed in me and pushed me when I needed to be pushed. She was a friend as well as a coach."

Shannon Miller: "My coach never stressed winning so much. He would always tell me before the meet to go out there and hit my routines and to 'have fun out there.' He never walked away. Whether I did really well or did really bad, he was by my side the entire time. That told me that he really cared about me not just about winning."

All of these gymnasts have clearly been successful. Their relationships with their coaches contributed to their success and allowed them to feel supported throughout their training.

One of the most important ways to make your training and relationship with your coaches successful is to listen carefully to your coaches. Gymnastics can be a risky sport, and it's normal to be scared of many skills you learn. When you are learning something new, it is important to trust your coach. No good coach would ask you to do something you are not prepared to do. If you don't trust your coach, you might hold back or chicken out in the middle when you go for a skill. If you aren't going for something completely, you can land wrong or even get hurt.

At the same time, you will want to be able to talk to your coaches. If you are concerned about how you are training or about an injury, you must be able to have an open conversation with your coach. A coach will not know about a problem unless you tell him or her. When Amanda Borden first began training with Mary Lee Tracy, Amanda did not always communicate her concerns. That led to some misunderstandings, but as Amanda got older, she was able to say, "I'm not feeling good today, and I'm afraid if I do any more, I'll get hurt." That way she and her coach could decide to back off on training for the day. Or she might say, "My ankle is hurting, but I can keep going." In this case, her coach could push her a little more through the end of workout. With good, two-way communication, an athlete and coach can jointly come to some decisions about how to handle a situation.

Although coaches will require hard work and sometimes are firm with their athletes, you want a coach who is positive as well. Everyone needs to hear positives, and most of us function much better when complimented. For instance, Bela Karolyi is known as a stern taskmaster but he also offers encouragement. Kerri Strug discussed how he balanced these two components: "[He] demanded discipline and lots of repetition. This paid off in competitions. Bela gave lots of positive comments and motivating words (and actions) prior to his athletes competing. This fired you up and gave you the extra level of confidence."

A good coach also knows when not to coach. Peter Vidmar's coach, Mako Sakamoto, sometimes did not say much during a workout. Mako knew that Peter had a lot of internal motivation and would be the first to recognize his own errors. When Mako did give suggestions or advice, it was sure to be important, and Peter knew to listen carefully.

Good coaches can play a big role in teaching many lessons, about both gymnastics and life. Coaches can help gymnasts learn how hard work and perseverance pay off. Coaches can help gymnasts desire success for themselves, not for anyone else. In addition, coaches can instill confidence in their athletes. So learn from your coach, and let him or her learn about you.

Coaches also can be a source of stress for gymnasts. Coaches can push too hard or require an intensity from the athlete that the gymnast does not feel. Some coaches forget to be positive and enthusiastic or forget that gymnasts are dealing with other life pressures of growing up. Gymnasts need to communicate their needs to their coaches, and coaches need to listen.

Parents will want to observe the relationship between their child and the coach. Often the relationship is good, with ample positive comments from the coach and open communication, but sometimes parents (or the gymnast) will not be satisfied with the coach's interactions. In this case, parents might find it

Co-head coach Scott Bull, UCLA, spotting former Bruin Denise Stott

useful to talk with the coach about their concerns. Approaching the coach in a non-threatening manner is always a good way to begin one of these conversations. Parents can begin by noting a positive aspect of the program or coach's work with their child. Then parents might mention that they have noticed certain behaviors (be specific) and are concerned about how this might affect their son or daughter. Finally parents can focus on working on a solution with the coaches. For instance, if a parent is concerned that the coach is not providing enough positive comments, the conversation might go something like this: "Coach, I wanted to let you know that Courtney is really learning a lot from you and improving all the time. We really appreciate all the work you do with her. . . . She looks up to you and is so pleased when you say positive things to her and notice her improvements. Lately she seems to need more of that from you. I was wondering if you might be able to offer her some more encouragement during her workouts. I know it would mean a lot to her." If the coach is responsive, then you may have said enough. If the coach is not responsive, you may need to be clearer about your needs. For instance, "It is important to me that Courtney participate in a program where there are ample positive comments about what she does. Will that be possible in your program?" Through a discussion like this, you can get a feel for whether the coach can offer the type of encouragement you want your child to have. If it seems unlikely, then you may have to consider changing programs. Remember that any concerns you have cannot be resolved if you do not talk about them. A good coach will work with you the best he or she can to come to some resolution. So start with communicating your thoughts and feelings before making any major decisions.

Whatever type of program your child pursues, it is important to look for good coaches. Refer to the checklist below for characteristics of a good coach:

- Has good technical knowledge

- Has good experience in coaching gymnastics

- Communicates well with gymnasts and parents

- Gives positive comments when the gymnast performs well

- Corrects mistakes in an encouraging and helpful manner

- Balances challenge and support as he or she trains the gymnast

- Is concerned more about the gymnast as an individual than about winning or losing

- Is sensitive to the gymnast's needs—doesn't over- or under-coach.

Clearly you will spend a lot of time with your coaches and get to know them well, but there will be many other people who become involved in your gymnastics career, and you may or may not know it. They are the fans and the media. Many of your fans you will know as friends and family, but others may simply admire you. Depending on the level you reach, the media may share your performances with countless other people. The next chapter helps you understand how to handle all these other people.

22

COPING WITH THE AUDIENCE, FANS, AND MEDIA

Clearly, gymnastics training and competitions occur in the public eye. From the smallest gyms to the most recognized international competitions, there are often spectators observing. Many gymnasts thrive on their public performances. They love to play to the crowd and involve the audience in their performances. Giving a performance like that can be a real "high." Also, sometimes being observed gives you that extra little push to move your performance up a notch. If performing in front of people is a motivating factor for you, GREAT! Hold onto that.

Other gymnasts may find that dealing with pressures and expectations from observers, fans, and the media is stressful for them. You don't have to be a high-level, well-known gymnast to experience these types of pressures. Gymnasts of all levels perform in front of other people and can gather fans and supporters. Although it can be flattering to have other people interested in you, it also can make you feel pressure to live up to other people's expectations.

The pressures you feel from other people are a type of anxiety. You'll remember that when we discussed anxiety in chapter 5, you learned that you can't avoid anxiety but must learn to cope with it. The same goes for pressures from fans or the media, or from both groups. You can't avoid the public nature of your performances and the fact that people will watch you. You have to find ways of dealing with these pressures.

Block out the pressures. One way to cope with these pressures is to learn how to block them out and ignore them. You can use the same types of focusing strategies we talked about using on events like beam (chapter 13) to prevent yourself from being distracted. It helps to practice with the pressure and distraction of others observing you as if you were in a meet. We call this *competition simulation*. You can do this in a variety of ways. You or your coach can ask everyone in the gym to stop and watch your routine. You can have others shout the types of comments you might hear while you are competing or have people take pictures of you while you perform. This way you experience training under the same conditions in which you compete. (See chapter 18 for more on simulating competitions.)

Perform for yourself. Another way to deal with being observed is to refocus on your personal goals. Rather than trying to live up to anyone else's expectations for you, decide what your goals are for yourself. Don't concern yourself with whether you might disappoint a friend or fan. Keep the focus on you. Amanda Borden says, "I don't feel or don't let those pressures get to me. The only pressure I feel is from myself. I expect perfection!" In addition, Amanda's coach taught the gymnasts to "go to the Olympic Trials because we wanted to make it, not for our parents, coaches or to be on TV. We dedicated ourselves to the sport because we wanted it for ourselves." Likewise, Shannon Miller says, "Most of the pressure I feel comes from within. I'm a perfectionist in everything I do."

As you can see from the above quotes, many Olympians have high expectations of themselves, and their desires to achieve come from within. It is important to realize that not

Kiralee Hayashi

every gymnast will have such high expectations or feel the need to be perfect. It's okay not to be perfect. In fact, it is next to impossible except for a very few. So decide what is realistic for you, and then perform for yourself.

Realize what you can and can't control. The only person you really have control over is yourself. You can't control the thoughts and actions of anyone else. There will be many people you come in contact with throughout your gymnastics career. Many will be supportive and helpful. Some will not be what you need. Realize that you can't control what people will do, but you can control whether you associate with helpful people. Kerri Strug emphasizes this point when she says,

> Just try and keep things in perspective. You can only do so much. You have to do what you can and not stress about the rest (things you can't control). This has taken me forever to learn, and I still sometimes lose perspective.

As you can see, learning about what you can and can't control is difficult, even for the best gymnasts. So don't be too hard on yourself if sometimes you don't reach your goals. Look at it as a learning experience; determine what you can control and work hard on that. Try to minimize the influence of the things over which you have little to no control.

Don't put too much stock in public opinions. Some gymnasts have the distinction of becoming well-known and facing an onslaught of public attention. For female gymnasts this often occurs at a young age, and the pressures can be enormous. For instance, when the U.S. women's team won the gold medal in the 1996 Olympics, all sorts of media discussion resulted. There were many public opinions about whether Kerri Strug should have attempted her second vault. There was discussion about what the entire team should do next with their newfound fame. Should the gymnasts train for further international competitions, go on tour, or attend college? No matter what choice each gymnast made, someone was going to disagree. So, after considering options, each gymnast had to do what was right for her. Even less known gymnasts will deal with others' opinions. You must learn to strike a balance between considering helpful input from others and making choices that are right for you.

It is important to find people you trust, who really care about your well-being, whom you can talk things over with. Usually these people would be your parents and coaches. You'll want to agree on your goals with your parents and coach(es), and then stick to them. This way you can focus less on what other outsiders have to say about your gymnastics career.

DEALING WITH FEAR

Case: Once there was a boy who loved gymnastics. One day in workout, his coach said, "Okay, today we are going to learn a double back off high bar." The boy's heart leapt into his throat as he thought about how scary that trick was. He spent a lot of time avoiding his coach that day in the hopes that his coach would forget about that double back. When it finally came to the fateful moment (because a good coach never forgets!), the boy decided to trust his coach and throw the double back. He made it, and he was on cloud nine! Even so, every workout after that, he was afraid of high bar dismounts, but he didn't give up and always worked with his fear. That boy was Peter Vidmar, 1984 Olympic Gold Medalist.

All gymnasts deal with fear. There is nothing wrong with being afraid. Being afraid merely reflects the respect you have for the difficult moves you are trying to perform, and you need the adrenaline that fear produces to perform the harder tricks. So you can't avoid fear; it's what you do with the fear that matters. You can allow it to direct what you do, or you can take charge of it and manage it.

23

OVERCOMING MENTAL BLOCKS

Case: Julie had done a back tuck on the beam countless times with her coach spotting and countless more times with him just standing there. She felt confident and knew she could do it. But the minute he stepped away and said, "Okay, do it yourself!" she froze. She physically could not make herself do it. Something stopped her, and her feet would not leave the beam. Her coach walked closer and stood right by her, and she did it. He walked away, and she could not. She became frustrated with herself, knowing she could do it but failing to get her body to respond.

We call this a mental block. Most gymnasts have experienced one (or more) of these as they try to learn new tricks. Mental blocks can be one of the most frustrating aspects of training. You pull out of a vault you know you can do. You can do the double back into the pit but not on a regular mat, or like Julie, you can't make yourself go for a skill that you can easily do. Julie is capable of doing the back tuck on the beam, but her mind gets in the way.

Often mental blocks occur because a gymnast thinks too much. The mind actually gets in the way of the body's ability to do what it knows how to do. For instance, instead of just throwing a skill, the gymnast starts thinking about all the possible ways to injure him- or herself. In Julie's case, the minute the coach said, "Okay, do it by yourself," she began thinking about how easily she could miss her foot. Once she had that picture in her mind, all she could do was stand there with her arms in the air. It felt as if there were steel bolts attaching her feet to the beam. Her feet simply would not move. This would have been a good time for Julie to use positive imagery. Instead of focusing on her legs being bolted to the beam, she could imagine her legs feeling like pistons that could propel her off the beam and through the air.

Another type of mental block is losing a skill that a gymnast has previously performed alone or even in competition. Most gymnasts have experienced this type of block too. One day the gymnast feels a little disoriented and doesn't throw the double full on floor quite right, or maybe her timing is off. She starts twisting too early off the ground and doesn't know where she is in the air. From there, things deteriorate until she can't do the skill at all. Coming into the gym the next day, all she can think about is how hard it was to get the double full right. She says to herself, "I hope I don't mess it up today." But she struggles again. The next day she has psyched herself out before she even tries the double full. We know she has the physical skills because she has done it countless times before, but now the mental component is preventing her from doing what she could previously do.

It is not uncommon to have trouble with a skill once it is learned. Sometimes if a gymnast leaves the skill alone for a time, she can come back renewed. The challenge occurs when she or her coaches pressure her to keep doing it. She ends up doing it this new, incorrect way, and that is what she practices. She loses confidence in her ability to do it correctly and becomes continually frustrated. She begins to have a negative association any time she thinks of practicing that skill.

How can you work with a mental block? How you deal with a mental block from the start can make a huge difference in how you get past it. If you or your coaches make a big deal about it, chances are it will be harder to get over, but if you recognize that blocks occur, relax, and work toward gradually overcoming it, you'll have better success. Also, take a look at these strategies.

1. First, get off the equipment and walk away to the side. Take a few deep breaths and relax. Think about what is getting in the way of your ability to perform the trick.

2. If fear of injury is the block, think about how unrealistic the possibility of injury is. Of course, any time you throw your body upside down in the air, intending to land upright, injury is a possibility. But gymnasts do hundreds of gymnastics moves a day and do not get injured. So, given your skills and your coach's confidence that you can do the move on your own, how likely is it that you will get injured? If you are ready for a skill, injury is unlikely, so begin visualizing successful completions of that trick. In addition, begin using positive self-talk to replace the negative thinking. (See chapter 7.)

3. If you tend to think too much, it may be easiest to get off the equipment, relax your mind, and get back on without thinking. Just allow your body to do what comes naturally. Practice imagery and feel your body doing the trick perfectly.

4. Think about something else before attempting the trick (although not to the degree that you are not paying attention to what you are doing). For instance, you might try listening to motivating music or doing mental math (count backward from 100 by 7s).

5. Talk to your coach and teammates. They may be able to offer some encouraging suggestions that they have found helpful, or they may be able to distract you so that you won't think too much. Remember not to blindly accept every suggestion you hear. You have to evaluate each comment to see

how relevant it is for you. Just because you ask for advice and get it, this does not mean you have to use it if it doesn't fit for you. So be selective in what you choose to use.

6. Give yourself rewards for overcoming a mental block. When you get frustrated with your inability to do a skill you've done before, it is tempting to punish yourself, but punishment is never as effective as reward. Punishment only reduces your self-esteem and frustrates you further. Peter Vidmar remembers an example of what not to do. When he was having difficulty letting go of the high bar for dismounts one day, he made a deal with one of his teammates (and with himself). He had a prized warm-up suit that he had received during an international competition, and he said to his teammate, "If I don't let go this next try, I'll give you the warm-up." Peter did not let go and never saw the warm-up suit again. Looking back, Peter realized that threatening himself did not help him get past his block.

A poor coach also will sometimes rely on punishment or humiliation as a means of trying to get an athlete over a mental block. Rarely does this type of coaching approach prove to be effective. When Karen Cogan was first learning gymnastics, one of the other athletes could not go for a back handspring on the beam, a trick she could easily do. The coach made her stand on the beam in the middle of the gym and hold a rubber chicken. She had to say, "I am a chicken" a number of times while everyone in the gym stopped what they were doing and watched her. Because this gym was in the middle of a YMCA, other people from other programs were walking through and stopped to watch. Through tears and nervous laughter she held the chicken and sang "the chicken song." The only thing this technique accomplished was to make her feel thoroughly humiliated. In fact, not long after that, she left gymnastics.

Positive incentives, on the other hand, will push you in the right direction. So make a list of treats for yourself. Treats could be anything—a bubble bath, a massage, a CD, a trip to the mall, allowing yourself time to read a good book, or a meal out at your favorite restaurant, to name just a few. When you succeed and work through a block, or even if you reach small goals in working toward getting past the block, give yourself a reward from the list.

7. Start over with small steps. Good coaches will take you through progressions as you learn a new skill. They don't tell you to throw a double back on floor before you learn a single back tuck. When working your way up to a skill, you do drills and develop the skills over time. If you develop a mental block, you might have to go back to some of the basics and work your way up again.

8. If you have tried many of these suggestions and still feel blocked, you may have to leave the trick for a while. Come back to it later that day or the next day.

9. You also can consult with a sport psychologist. This professional will help you examine what is causing the mental block and assist you in overcoming it.

10. Use imagery. In several chapters we have discussed imagery to improve performance. Imagery is extremely useful for overcoming mental blocks. Imagine yourself doing the skill perfectly and fearlessly. Do this over and over until it becomes second nature. Continue to imagine this skill in and out of the gym.

Think about the gymnast having trouble with a double full (described earlier in this chapter). Here are some things she can do:

a. Take a day off from working double fulls.
b. Watch a video of herself doing double fulls incorrectly to understand what she needs to change; then watch a video of herself (or someone else) doing them correctly to imprint correct technique in her mind.
c. Start over with her progressions. Make a checklist of elements to master. For instance, work layouts, then fulls, then double fulls again.

 d. Get a spot to get the correct timing back.

 e. Use the pit to experiment with changing her technique.

 f. Use positive imagery.

One of the causes of mental blocks is fear of injury; thinking too much about injury can paralyze you. Injuries themselves pose a number of challenges for gymnasts. The next chapter is devoted to an examination of injury in gymnastics.

Luisa Portocarerro

24

CONCERNS ABOUT INJURIES

Tim Daggett, 1984 Olympic Gold Medalist, experienced a very serious injury the year before the 1988 Olympics. He had had a number of prior injuries, the most serious of which was a ruptured disk in his neck after a fall off high bar. He battled his way back in only nine months from that injury, only to get mononucleosis during the Pan American games in July 1987. He again got past that obstacle and was competing in September 1987 in the world championships in Rotterdam, Holland. He did well on some events and had a shot at finals. He got through rings, which was difficult due to the previous neck injury, and he felt very positive about his performances. He had a good compulsory score on vault and was up last for the United States. He had a shot at vault finals and in his positive frame of mind aggressively went after vault. In the air he twisted too early and was crooked. He twisted on the landing and severely fractured his leg. "I had no idea what happened, it wasn't [didn't feel like] my leg. The tibia was sticking straight forward," he said.

At the hospital, he was told he could potentially lose his leg. He had severed an artery and had lost a lot of blood. He also developed compartment syndrome and had surgery to relieve the pressure. A Dutch physician told him that his gymnastics career was over, and a good goal would be to have a working leg.

For a long time he felt depressed and cheated. He had learned early that success required dedication, commitment, and sacrifices. He had prided himself on being an extremely hard worker throughout his gymnastics career. If he came up against roadblocks, he worked past them. He had done everything right. Then why was he now being told he couldn't beat this injury? None of it made sense.

The depression he felt was difficult to get past—one second he could do anything (as he ran down to vault); the next, he could do nothing. After two weeks in a Dutch hospital, he was flown home and was met at the UCLA Medical Center by Dr. Bert Mandelbaum, who said, "Timmy, you'll be fine, and you'll go to the Olympics again." In his depressed frame of mind, Tim didn't believe Dr. Mandelbaum. Every day was a challenge. For every other injury, Tim had been in the gym the next day. He had even competed in Japan with a cast! This time he was a self-admitted uncooperative and unmotivated patient.

After he went home, he had a full-time nursing assistant. The nurse would push him in the wheelchair outside while he passively went along for the ride. One day he decided to move the wheelchair up a hill himself. He almost fell into the road, but insisted on no help and made it to the top! He realized that working back from this injury was the same as coming back from previous injuries, and now he had a goal. He did not have to quit or give up.

The "experts" said he could not come back from this injury, but at the 1988 Olympic Trials, he was eighth in the All Around after the first day of competition, and he had won two events. He eventually pulled out of the Olympic Trials due to concerns about reinjuring his leg, but he says, "I am more proud of what I did after 1984 [Olympics]. I hold that in higher regard [than the Olympic accomplishments]."

Injury is a risk of any sport, and gymnastics is certainly no exception. It is not difficult to recognize that all the aerial moves leave many chances for error. Gymnasts are prone to any type of stress injury—shin splints, ankle sprains, shoulder strains (especially men). On very rare occasions, some even experience severe head or neck injuries, or both. It is not surprising that the fear of injury often gets in the way of optimal performance. Once injured, gymnasts then deal with the fear of reinjury. Sometimes the fear of reinjury becomes realistic: being too tentative and thinking too much about what you can do wrong can lead to a reinjury.

When any athlete gets injured, the focus is usually on rehabilitating the injury physically. It is common to think that once athletes are physically healed, they are ready to jump right back into the sport again, but injury often results in many psychological effects. The athlete may have doubts, fears, and anxieties that make returning to a full practice particularly difficult. Often the fear is related to the risk of getting reinjured. When an injury occurs, especially if it is severe, a gymnast's worst fears have come true. Then the athlete must work with him- or herself to get back in the gym and try the same skill as well as other skills again.

Causes of injury. Sometimes injuries occur because of a fluke. The gymnast took off a little too low or got lost in the air. Sometimes injuries occur because the gymnast is not really ready to try a new skill but does anyway. Often, psychological factors make it more likely that injury will occur. One factor related to injury is the number and degree of stressful life events that have happened recently to a gymnast. For example, a death in the family or parents' getting divorced would be stressful life events. Sometimes life events are positive but are still stressful, such as moving to a new home, having a new baby born in a family, or beginning to train at a new gym. The greater the number of stressful life events an athlete experiences, the greater the risk of injury.

Having the support of friends and family can be helpful in coping with stressful life events, but if an athlete does not have support from family and friends, he or she may have more difficulty handling stress. The risk of injury is also increased without support.

Effects of injury. Gymnasts will view injury in different ways. Some will see even a moderate injury as disastrous because it takes them out of practice for ten days. Others might see the injury as an opportunity to show courage and work on rehabilitation. Still others might see it as a welcome break from intense workouts.

Gymnasts will likely have a number of emotional reactions to the injury, most notably fear and anxiety. Gymnasts can become distracted when they spend much of their mental energy focusing on this fear and anxiety. Then reinjuries or other new injuries are more likely. Focusing on the injury (e.g., thinking about what you did wrong instead of how to do it correctly) also can lead to lowered confidence or lowered motivation, or both. In addition, a gymnast is likely to feel disappointed, especially if the injury takes the athlete out of gymnastics for a long time during rehabilitation or even out of the sport permanently. She or he may feel depressed if the rehabilitation takes months and becomes tedious. In fact, the injury may seem as if it will never heal.

Dealing with injury. Below are some strategies to assist gymnasts as they come back from an injury.

1. First, follow your medical doctor's advice and do all of the prescribed physical therapy or rehabilitation. Be sure to communicate with your physician or physical therapist, or both, to get all of your questions answered. These professionals are there to make your recovery as effective as possible. Take care of the injury physically. At the same time, begin turning to the emotional healing as outlined below.

2. Get support. Some gymnasts may prefer to handle the injury without talking about it much. They may be able to treat the injury and also plan for full reentry into the gym on their own. This might be especially likely with minor injuries. Others may need to talk about their disappointments or fears as they deal with this new change in their training schedule. Whatever your need, it is usually helpful to get some type of support and encouragement for get-

ting through the rehabilitation phase. You may need to ask people for support if they are not aware you need it. Don't be afraid to talk to people who can help such as your trainer, physical therapist, or physician. That's what they are there for.

3. Practice even when you can't. "How do you practice when you are injured?" you might ask. An injury is the perfect time to practice mentally. If a gymnast cannot practice physically, why not do the next best thing? Use mental imagery. Mentally visualizing skills and routines can keep you in the gym more than you think. Research shows that mental practice is more effective than no practice at all (Feltz & Landers, 1983), so it certainly can't hurt to add mental practice to your rehabilitation routine. In addition, use imagery to experience successful performances of the skill on which you were injured. It is easy to lose confidence for performing a skill just after an injury. So work toward regaining your confidence by visualizing positive outcomes.

   Amanda Borden has had a lot of injuries during her gymnastics career. During those times when she couldn't train physically, she trained mentally. She went to each event and did her routines mentally. She even made a "workout tape" that she would use to visualize everything she would do in workout as well as during the Olympic Trials. Injuries don't have to prevent you from becoming an Olympic Champion.

4. Use imagery to heal your injury. Just as the power of your mind can help you maintain your skills, it can also speed physical healing. You can imagine the injured area recovering, the ligaments growing together and strengthening, the bone depositing more calcium and healing the crack, or the fluids that cause the swelling flushing out of the joint. It doesn't matter that you don't know what healing really looks like, just that you focus the power of your mind on the injured area and envision a healing/strengthening process taking place.

Sample Script: Find a comfortable, quiet place, and close your eyes. Begin breathing deeply and relaxing your body, using the exercises you have learned in previous chapters of this book. Then picture the injured area of your body (joint, bone, ligament, rip). Focus on what it might look like inside (a cracked bone, torn ligaments), whatever that looks like to you. Take a few moments to see the details of how the bones and tendons of the injured area fit together inside of you. Now begin to picture healing taking place. See the fibers in your ligaments growing back together and becoming stronger (or see calcium deposits bringing the cracked bone together or see the skin on a rip or incision healing). See the fluids that have made that area swollen flushing out of your system and taking with them any pain. Envision blood flowing to the injured area and bringing nutrients to speed healing while taking away any debris or pain. Focus on this healing process for a few moments, examining the details of your body working for you and begin to imagine the injury healing to its original state. After you have completed this imagery, take a few moments to remain relaxed and open your eyes when you are ready.

5. Use positive self-talk. Just as you visualize positive outcomes to your skills, you will want to say positive things to yourself to enhance your performance. You will want to say things like "I know I can come back and do this skill again." You also can increase your confidence by reminding yourself of your positive attributes and gymnastics abilities.

6. Set goals for recovery. Use the goal-setting strategies you learned in chapter 9 to set reasonable goals for your recovery. Just as you set goals to learn a new skill, you can set short-term goals with target dates to progress through your rehabilitation. For instance, after Karen Cogan tore ligaments in her knee, she set goals to achieve increasing range of motion in that joint (or how far she could bend her knee). Her first goal was 30 degrees, then 60 degrees, then 90 degrees. Each week the trainer measured the degrees she could bend her knee until she regained full range of motion. Having a number to shoot for gave Karen the incentive to push through some difficult rehabilitation exercises.

7. Make a comeback step by step. It can be frustrating and disappointing when you first try to do gymnastics again after having been out of physical practice for a while. Even if you have been doing physical conditioning and the prescribed rehabilitation exercises, you still may feel weak in some ways, or your timing may be off, or both. Your mind may know how to do skills, but your body is lagging behind. Again, set reasonable goals for yourself and reward your progress. Keep in mind that how quickly you come back depends on the severity of the injury, your commitment to your rehabilitation program, and your level of confidence, to name a few. In addition, you must follow medical advice as you ease back in. Tim Daggett's severe injury took months of rehabilitation before he could regain his pre-injury health. Remember to take it slow and go step by step.

8. Avoid isolation. It might be easy to stay away from the gym and your teammates when you are injured and can't do much gymnastics, but it is important to stay involved with training and your friends. So make an appearance as often as you can and do as much as you can, remembering to follow your physician's orders. Even if it is only walking around on crutches or doing a few chin-ups and sit-ups (remember, you are strengthening those muscles, and it will help you later), staying involved in some way will help you maintain motivation as you start on the road to recovery.

9. Start with the basics. In chapter 2 we discussed starting with the basics. Now again, you will be starting with the basics, and it might seem like starting over. The good news is that your skills will come back faster than it took to learn them in the first place. But you need to build strength and stamina and become familiar with gymnastics again. With hard work and perseverance, you can get to where you were and even surpass your pre-injury abilities.

Preventing injuries and dealing effectively with them when they happen are ways of keeping your body healthy. Maintaining a positive body image and practicing good eating habits are other important ways of maintaining your physical and mental health. The next section examines these issues in depth.

DEALING WITH BODY IMAGE AND EATING CONCERNS

Body image and eating concerns are a prime focus in gymnastics. With the emphasis on being small and powerful, it is nearly impossible for gymnasts to avoid a substantial awareness of their bodies and an understanding of how size and diet contribute to performance. The next two chapters examine body and eating concerns. You will find strategies for maintaining health in gymnastics while facing these issues.

25

BODY IMAGE AND AWARENESS

Take a moment and picture what the top male and female gymnasts in the world look like. What do you see? For females, you likely see a short, small, strong, thin/lean, but muscularly defined young girl. For men, you probably still see short and strong, but older (college aged) with more powerful muscle definition. For females rather than males, thin is an expectation.

Body type, for female gymnasts especially, has evolved over the past three decades. In the 1960s, gymnasts looked like women, with defined breasts and hips, even though they were lean. Vera Caslavska was 5' 3" and 121 pounds when she won the 1968 Olympics at the age of 26. In the 1972 Olympics, Olga Korbut demonstrated how successful a smaller gymnast could be. At the 1976 Olympics, a tiny 14-year-old, Nadia Comaneci, achieved perfect 10s. Everyone began to realize that small and young were a winning combination. From there, elite gymnasts have become smaller and younger. Although there are no official limitations on height and weight, the unofficial expectation for international competition now seems to be gymnasts who are under 5 feet tall and under 90 pounds. For instance, Shannon Miller was 4' 10" and 79 pounds when she won the

1993 Worlds at age 16. If a gymnast is trying to fit that mold, most will be past their prime before age 17 or 18. That is why we rarely see female gymnasts qualify for two Olympic teams in a row, and if we do, it is usually with a more mature body.

For boys and men, the pressures to attain a certain body type are different. Of course, lean is expected, but male gymnasts also need an incredible amount of strength. Prior to adolescence, boys will have particular difficulty performing on events, like rings, that require upper body strength. Boys aim towards more muscular development as opposed to thinness.

At an early age, most gymnasts become aware of their bodies and outward appearance. Body appearance is often a focus of conversation among young gymnasts, especially females, as they are training. Because the "uniform" is a leotard, there is no place to hide any excess weight. Gymnasts are aware of others' looking them up and down and know that observers compare body types and sizes among gymnasts.

Aspiring female gymnasts may see small, young Olympic competitors and strive to attain (or maintain) such body proportions. Girls may think their bodies must look a particular way in order for them to be successful. Although some girls may be able to stay naturally small and thin, the majority cannot. Most are fighting genetics and normal physical developmental patterns. Girls are meant to grow into women with the accompanying changes in body shape and size. The unreasonable expectation of thinness can (a) put undue pressure on the gymnast to achieve an unrealistic body type and (b) result in an excessive focus on physical appearance. These conditions increase the risk that young female gymnasts will try to lose weight in unhealthy ways to achieve a specific body type and subsequently develop eating disorders. Eating disorders will be discussed in more detail in the next chapter.

Fortunately, we see positive examples of how gymnasts deal with their growth. Shannon Miller, an Olympian in 1992 and 1996, commented on the usefulness of being taller for the 1996 Olympics: "When I grew about 4 inches in '93, I didn't let it hinder my performance. Instead I used the extra height and weight to create more power, for higher and more difficult vaulting and tumbling." Amanda Borden grew four inches in one year as well "and lost all of my skills. It was very frustrating, but you have to learn how to handle it. You do have to be stronger and your timing is different, but if you push through it, I think you're actually stronger." In addition, Svetlana Boginskaya was successful in three Olympics (1988, 1992, and 1996) even though by the 1996 Olympics she was taller and older than most other gymnasts. So the extra height and weight from normal growth do not have to prevent you from reaching your potential. You just have to learn to work with them.

There is also another way to look at body type: If you watch any NCAA meets, you will see that there are a variety of body types among the successful collegiate gymnasts. In fact, many of the top female college gymnasts have become muscular and powerful as opposed to excessively thin. Karen Cogan remembers the very healthy attitudes of gymnasts with whom she competed in college. They would say things like "I might not be thin for a gymnast, but I look great compared to the rest of the population. I refuse to diet or pick up unhealthy eating habits." Those gymnasts were successful competitors and commanded respect from everyone else. As the women from the 1996 Olympic team continue to mature into young women, you will notice that they are still exceptional, powerful gymnasts.

From a psychological perspective, attempts to achieve a small, thin body type can be damaging. A gymnast who is not naturally small and thin may develop a negative body image. Even gymnasts who are small and thin may become dissatisfied with their bodies and attempt to achieve what they view as even greater perfection. "Perfection" usually translates into "thinner" (and unhealthy). When any type of dissatisfaction kicks in, a gymnast is likely to view her body negatively, even to the point of developing an intense dislike for her body. Perceived fat and dissatisfaction may be related to negative thinking, less confidence, and low self-esteem. Often gymnasts may become frustrated by the inability to change their body size and shape, and they resort to unhealthy means of regulating weight to achieve such a physique.

Gymnasts can benefit from becoming comfortable with their bodies. Rather than focusing on the thighs that are just slightly bigger than she thinks they should be or sucking her stomach in every moment, it is useful to focus on what she likes about her body. Maybe the strength she has developed in her legs allows her to leap high on beam or tumble high on floor, or maybe she has been working hard to increase arm strength and is beginning to see results. Look at how your body helps you in gymnastics rather than what is wrong with it.

You want to become comfortable with what you are and fight the obsession with body image. You don't need to look in the full-length mirror every time you pass by. You don't need to make constant comparisons with your teammates. You don't need to buy into unhealthy expectations of your body shape and size.

You'll probably enjoy gymnastics more if you focus on mastering skills rather than on where you carry one extra pound. Gymnastics can still be a terrific sport even if you are not 4'10" and 85 pounds. You can be successful in high school, college, or a more recreational program. Show everyone how good you can be in whatever arena you choose!

Gymnasts also can focus on developing feelings of self-worth in areas other than their bodies. If how you feel about yourself depends on how you think you look, then your self-esteem may be on a continuous roller-coaster ride. Spend some time evaluating other strengths you have. You might excel at school, might be a great friend, might easily demonstrate compassion or have other special talents outside of gymnastics. Don't forget about these other achievements and attributes when you think about or describe yourself.

At some point, you may even decide to retire from gymnastics or reduce your level of competitiveness. You have many goals you can pursue with a normal-sized body. Or you may never choose to train and compete intensively. Not all gymnastics is Olympic-level competition. "General gymnastics," a relatively new discipline, is for every age level (tots to seniors) and skill level. Activities include artistic, rhythmic, and acro gymnastics as well as marching, dance, cheerleading, diverse handicap movement, trampolining, calisthenics, and games. General gymnastics encourages cooperative learning and social interaction, fitness, and expression through movement. Further information is available by contacting USA Gymnastics.* General gymnastics is another alternative to consider so that you can continue to be active and involved in the sport. This way gymnastics can be a great sport for everyone.

Most gymnasts, both males and females, will become very aware of their body and develop a body image. Many gymnasts are able to maintain a healthy attitude about their bodies even with the many pressures they might feel. Some gymnasts, however, really struggle with their appearance, and can develop eating disorders. The next chapter examines what occurs when eating issues become unhealthy.

---

*Attention: General Gymnastics, USA Gymnastics, Pan American Plaza, Suite 300, 201 S. Capitol Ave, Indianapolis, IN 46225; phone: (317) 237-5050; email: gg@usa-gymnastics.org.

26

EATING DISORDERS

No discussion of body image in a sport like gymnastics would be complete without an examination of eating disorders. Most gymnasts do not suffer from diagnosable eating disorders (Petrie, 1993; Petrie & Stoever, 1993). They learn to accept their bodies and manage food in a healthy way. We encourage you to learn good eating practices right from the start of your career.

Eating disorders are dangerous, and the best way to avoid unhealthy eating patterns is to prevent them before they happen. Prevention can be done through education and knowledge, so this chapter presents useful information about eating disorders. This information is not presented to scare young gymnasts or parents but rather to inform readers about the seriousness of eating disorders and the need to get treatment if they do occur.

Let's start with an example.

When 14-year-old Andrea got home from workout, she went straight to the full-length mirror and looked at herself in her leotard. Her coach was right. She was gaining weight. She had been embarrassed when he pulled her aside and said she better watch what she was eating. She saw now the excess on her thighs and a slight bulge on her stomach. "That's it!" she thought to herself. "I'm going on a diet starting right now." She told her mother she was not hungry and skipped dinner that night. She began to cut out all high-fat foods and even cut down on portions of her regular meals. Soon she began counting calories obsessively and cutting out even more foods. She began to lose weight and was complimented by her coach and teammates. It felt good to set her mind on something and get results. So she kept counting calories, cutting down on her food intake until she became very thin. She began to feel light-headed, but assumed it was because she was training so hard. In fact, she felt in control of herself and thought her gymnastics was going better than ever. She continued to diet and lost even more weight. Soon she began having difficulty sleeping at night and would get up and exercise to pass the time. She felt weaker during workouts but assumed it was because she was exercising more. Soon workouts weren't going too well. She could not get through a floor routine, she felt tired after just warming up, and she was getting injured more because she couldn't get high enough in the air to do her skills. She also could not get through the usual conditioning training at the end of workout each day.

Now people were worried about her. Her parents had tried to encourage her to eat more, but she refused. She had heard some of her teammates whispering about how she looked ill. Even her coach was worried about her because she did not have the endurance she once had. People began to tell her she needed to gain weight and that she looked gaunt and tired all the time. She refused and continued to cut down on her food intake.

Struggles with food and weight, such as Andrea's, are too common in gymnastics. With body appearance being so central, it is no surprise that food and diet can become a focus in a gymnast's life. As very young athletes, gymnasts may have little difficulty maintaining an ideal weight because they are burning so much energy during hours of practice, but as their bodies go through the expected growth and changes of adolescence, they will find it more difficult to stay at what they think is an ideal weight. To maintain the lean, small stature, many gymnasts begin counting calories at an early age. Many adolescent girls then resort to strict dieting to prevent nature from taking its course with their bodies. Some studies even suggest that restricting caloric intake at a young age can stunt growth permanently. If a gymnast becomes frustrated with the lack of results from dieting, she may begin using unhealthy means of controlling her weight that are known as eating disorders.

There are two main types of eating disorders that affect gymnasts: anorexia nervosa and bulimia nervosa.

Anorexia nervosa (sometimes shortened to anorexia) means "a nervous loss of appetite." This definition does not accurately reflect what happens with anorexia because anorexics tend to have appetites and think about food constantly, but they do not allow themselves to eat. Anorexia involves the following symptoms as outlined in the American Psychiatric Association *Diagnostic and Statistical Manual IV* (*DSM-IV*; 1994):

- A refusal to maintain normal body weight for age and height. Typically, someone who weighs less than 85% of his or her expected body weight (which could include failure to gain weight during expected growth phases) would fit this criterion.

- Intense fear of gaining weight or becoming fat, even if underweight.

- A distorted view of how one's body looks, for instance, feeling fat while looking extremely thin or emaciated to everyone else.

- Amenorrhea (absence of menstrual cycles) in girls who have started (or should have started) their menstrual period. [Note that some gymnasts do not begin their menstrual cycles until after they "retire" from the sport.]

- Often these symptoms are accompanied by denial of (or unwillingness to admit to) the seriousness of the eating problem or weight loss.

Bulimia nervosa (often shortened to bulimia) literally means "ox hunger" according to *The American Heritage College Dictionary*. It is characterized by binge eating and purging and includes the following symptoms according to the *DSM-IV*:

- Episodes of binge eating, which means eating amounts of food in a short time period that are definitely larger than most people would eat during a similar time period. These episodes also involve a sense of lacking control and being unable to stop eating this much.

- Episodes of purging (getting rid of food) to compensate for so much food intake. Purging could take the form of self-induced vomiting, laxative use, diuretic use, fasting, or excessive exercise.

- The binge-and-purge cycle occurs on average twice a week for at least three months.

- The individual's view of her- or himself is overly influenced by body shape and weight.

Experts on eating disorders view eating behaviors on a continuum (e.g., Striegel-Moore et al., 1986). On one end are individuals who have no signs of disordered eating behaviors at all. On the other end are individuals with severe, diagnosable anorexia and bulimia. The majority of athletes fall somewhere between those two extremes and can exhibit some types of disordered eating behaviors without having a full-blown eating disorder. For instance, a gymnast might go through periods of excessive dieting, but not become anorexic, or a gymnast might have an occasional binge but not make a habit of it. Each of these behaviors is potentially troublesome, but by themselves would not mean the gymnast had an eating disorder.

Most people tend to view eating disorders as women's disorders. It is true that eating disorders affect more women than men; however, it is important to recognize that men also develop eating disorders. Especially in a sport like gymnastics where optimum weight is so important, men are susceptible to disordered eating as well.

It is unclear how many gymnasts are affected by eating disorders. Research on collegiate gymnasts indicates that 60% have engaged in "intermediate" (although not diagnosable) disordered-eating practices, and 16% use excessive exercise to control weight (Petrie, 1993). Studies on collegiate gymnasts also indicate that somewhere between 4% and 16% have diagnosable bulimia (Petrie, 1993; Petrie & Stoever, 1993); however, no statistics are available for the percentages of gymnasts who have diagnosable anorexia.

In the example at the beginning of this chapter, Andrea is showing signs of anorexia nervosa. She began dieting to help with her performance, and at first dieting was effective for her. Soon, however, she became overconcerned with her body weight. She began having difficulty with her endurance, strength, and energy level. Without endurance she will struggle to get through her routines, especially floor and bars, not to mention just getting through a workout. If Andrea keeps restricting her food intake and losing weight, the illness could become life threatening.

There are a number of physical and medical complications associated with eating disorders. Physical complications:

- dizziness and/or fainting

- dehydration

- tooth enamel loss and/or tooth decay

- hair loss

- electrolyte imbalance

- brittle nails

- diminished muscle mass

- intestinal problems

Electrolyte imbalances and dehydration due to diuretic and laxative use or failure to eat or drink can develop into severe conditions and become life threatening. Other medical complications, which also can be severe include:

- gastrointestinal bleeding

- heart arrhythmias

- difficulty absorbing fat, protein, and calcium

- tears in the esophagus

- anemia

- ulcers

If these conditions are allowed to persist, they can lead to death. Gymnasts have died from anorexia. Former U.S. national team member, Christy Henrich, developed anorexia and bulimia during her career and eventually died from multiple organ failure because of this self-starvation. According to *International Gymnast* magazine (October 1994), Henrich came into gymnastics prominence in the late 1980s, with her best competitive year being 1989, when she placed second at the USA championships. She was forced to retire in 1990, however, because her severe weight loss resulted in insufficient strength to perform her routines. She weighed 95 pounds during her competitive peak but was around 61 pounds when she died in 1994 at the age of 22. She had even dropped below 50 pounds just prior to her death. Sadly, no one was aware of her eating disorder until it had taken such a firm grip of her that it was out of control.

One medical concern involving disordered eating behaviors that has received attention lately is the Female Athlete Triad. Female Athlete Triad, as defined by the American College of Sports Medicine (1997), consists of (a) disordered eating, (b) amenorrhea (lack of menstrual periods), and (c) premature osteoporosis (early bone loss). Female Athlete Triad is of particular concern for gymnasts because of the high risk of developing disordered eating patterns, which may lead to delayed or discontinued menstrual periods and subsequent osteoporosis. Currently, there is not enough research to determine the likelihood that gymnasts will develop osteoporosis because their muscle development actually creates positive bone mass and bone density. Until the research is clearer, however, gymnasts need to be aware of the possibility of osteoporosis.

Eating disorders are very serious psychological illnesses that have physical ramifications. In other words, eating disorders are not really about food. Usually eating disorders evolve for a variety of reasons, which could include the need to maintain control, family conflicts, low self-esteem, perfectionistic tendencies, and societal pressures. Food and weight are the ways these psychological issues manifest themselves.

A sport like gymnastics creates an environment that puts athletes at risk for developing eating disorders. Factors that place gymnasts at risk:

- Emphasis on appearance. Because body appearance is so central to gymnastics, athletes may feel pressure to maintain what they consider an optimal weight. They may perceive that a certain appearance will lead to success.

- Pressure from adults. Coaches, parents, or other officials may put pressure on gymnasts to maintain an arbitrarily determined weight range. This pressure might be unintentional or subtle, although in some cases it may even be very obvious. Gymnasts are very sensitive to weight issues and easily can pick up on cues about their appearance.

- Perfectionistic tendencies. Gymnasts are likely to be somewhat perfectionistic. If they weren't, they probably would not achieve their goals, but perfectionism is also one characteristic that goes along with eating disorders.

- Low self-esteem. Adolescence in girls is associated with a reduction in self-esteem (AAUW, 1991). Combine that with coaching environments in which criticism about performance and appearance abounds, and you have a dangerous combination. In addition, criticisms that are delivered through yelling or personal attacks (e.g., "You are awful. You'll never amount to anything!") can lower self-esteem.

The best way to deal with eating disorders is to prevent them before they happen, but how do you do that when there are so many pressures pushing young gymnasts in that direction? First, it is important to understand that we all have to learn to live with food because we can't survive without it. When people have trouble with alcohol, for instance, they can stop drinking and completely avoid their nemesis. We can't do that with eating. We have to strike a balance between healthy eating and weight management. We have to stay away from the extremes of starving or binging. Instead, we must find ways of using food and exercise to help us become fit and energetic and, consequently, excel at gymnastics.

Dieting does *not* work. Goals to cut calories and lose weight only create an obsession with food that becomes counterproductive and can lead to eating disorders. A focus on eating nutritiously is more effective than counting calories. In fact, if you listen to what former Olympians say, you see the emphasis is on eating healthy rather than restricting food intake.

> Jaycie Phelps: "I never had a strict diet. I was just always careful with my fat intake and making sure I got enough protein, carb[ohydrate]s, and vitamins."

> Shannon Miller: "My parents and coaches have taught me how to eat nutritious foods. I don't diet; I just try to eat normal."

> Amanda Borden: "I always watch what I eat because I know how important it is to put good food into your body to fuel it."

Coaches and parents must learn to take the emphasis away from weight and body appearance. Sometimes weigh-ins are used to monitor a gymnast's weight. Routine weigh-ins are a dangerous setup for eating disorders and should be avoided in the interest of the gymnast's long-term health. If weigh-ins are determined to be necessary, it is best to put someone besides the coaches and parents in charge of them. An athletic trainer or physician can play this role. At most, weight should be recorded once or twice a year to establish a baseline and chart healthy growth patterns. Other than that, there should be a good reason to check weight, such as the need to monitor dehydration during intense summer workouts. Weigh-ins should always be done with each athlete individually in private, and coaches should never post athlete weights in public.

Weight should be considered only in the context of a gymnast's normal growth and development. All female gymnasts will grow into women with their bodies changing accordingly. Growth is normal, and a gymnast should not be criticized for it. Height and weight do not have to be a hindrance to successful gymnastics performances. In chapter 25, some of the 1996 Olympians discussed changes in their bodies. Their attitudes about changes in their bodies were positive, and they were able to find ways to work with their growth.

Coaches and parents need to be aware that permanent damage can occur with restricting caloric intake and should discourage any excessive dieting before it gets out of hand. Gyms can teach healthy, balanced eating and bring in nutritionists who understand the special needs of gymnasts. In short, forget the dieting and deal with weight by encouraging healthy eating. Think of food as an essential partner in your gymnastics success. You need protein for muscle development, carbohydrates for energy and endurance, and fat for energy. Often gymnasts think fat is to be completely avoided, but fat is not a bad thing. It actually is a very important part of your diet. Fat is an ideal fuel for your body because it provides the largest nutrient store of potential energy and can be easily converted into energy. During light and moderate exercise, fat contributes about 50% of the energy requirement, and during prolonged exercise fat contributes 80% of the body's energy needs. So you do not want to overdo your fat intake, but if you avoid fat completely, you will have very little energy, especially for prolonged exercise. Gymnasts can benefit by taking a healthy, realistic perspective on the use of fat in their diets.

Prevention of eating disorders is imperative, but even with the best prevention program, gymnasts still will struggle with eating disorders. Here are some strategies for managing eating concerns.

For gymnasts. If you are dealing with an eating disorder. . . .

1. The first step is to admit to yourself there is a problem and that you need help. Most anorexics deny that their eating habits are problematic and unhealthy. If you don't think there is a problem, you are not likely to get help. Bulimics usually recognize a problem but might be reluctant to get help. So look honestly at yourself, what you are doing, and what you might need.

2. Then confide in a trusted friend, coach, or parent. This person should be someone who will look out for your best interests and assist you in getting help.

3. Get counseling. Some disordered eating patterns are minor. A gymnast may be able to work on her own to alter habits once she knows the potential dangers involved and learns to eat correctly, but most of the time, eating disorders require professional help from a psychologist or therapist who specializes in treating eating disorders. It's even better if the therapist has knowledge of sport too. A good therapist can assist a gymnast in understanding the underlying psychological issues, getting past the eating disorder, and regaining healthy eating habits for gymnastics success.

4. Consult a nutritionist. A nutritionist (or registered dietician) can be useful as well because he or she will know about all necessary food groups to include in a diet. As with therapists, a nutritionist who understands athletes' special needs can be particularly helpful. He or she can work out an individualized eating plan for a gymnast so that the athlete maintains appropriate muscle development and body-fat percentage and gets adequate nutrition at the same time.

If you are a parent, friend, or coach of someone struggling with an eating disorder, remember that you cannot cure this person. Pressuring yourself to do so will only increase the stress both you and the gymnast feel. Also, it will not be useful to force the athlete to eat or to monitor his or her eating habits.

It is likely the gymnast will only rebel and become further entrenched in the disordered eating behaviors. The gymnast needs to become responsible for his or her own healing. But you *can* do the following:

1. Gather information. Determine what leads you to believe the gymnast has an eating disorder. Be ready to present specific behaviors to support what you believe. For instance, you may have noticed excessive weight loss or suspect vomiting. This is concrete "evidence" you can discuss with the gymnast.

2. Find out about resources. Determine what treatment options are available for the gymnast. If you know a sport psychologist or therapist, consult that individual for options. Also in some cities, there are often eating-disorder support groups available.

3. In a caring, gentle way, approach the gymnast with your concerns. Ask how the individual is doing in general; it is important to show you care about the athlete as a person. Then discuss the symptoms you have noticed. Focus on how worried you are and your concern that they could reflect an eating problem. You can offer to help him or her get treatment.

4. If the gymnast refuses to get help, and you are certain a problem exists, you must consider your options. If you are in a position of power (parent, coach), you can insist that the gymnast receive treatment, but remember the decision must come from genuine caring and concern. If you are the parent of a minor child, you are obligated to get help before the eating disorder gets out of hand. An experienced professional can help you once you decide to intervene. If you are the coach, you may need to place restrictions on the gymnast's ability to work out in the gym until he or she gets the needed help. Sometimes structured goals for treatment of an eating disorder and subsequent reentry into gymnastics training can be determined among a team of concerned professionals who might include parents, coaches, nutritionist, psychologist, and/or physician.

5. If you are not in a position to require that the gymnast seek treatment, you can continue to be available to the gymnast should she change her mind about needing help. You can support the gymnast as a person, but you do not have to support unhealthy eating behavior or attitudes. For instance, if you both have previously enjoyed going out to eat together, but now when you go out he or she refuses to eat, you might choose not to participate in any meals out with him or her.

If you would like more information about eating disorders, local support groups, and/or a referral to professionals in your area, please contact one of the following associations:

1. The National Association of Anorexia Nervosa and Associated Disorders (ANAD)
   Address: Box 7, Highland Park, IL 60035
   Hotline: 847-831-3438
   Fax: 847-433-4632
   Email: anad20@aol.com
   Online: http://www.healthtouch.com
   http://members.aol.com/anad20/index.html

2. Anorexia Nervosa and Related Eating Disorders, Inc. (ANRED)
   On-line: http://www.anred.com

Suggested Readings:

1. Dussere Farrell, M. (1995). *Athlete's cookbook*. Indianapolis, IN: Masters Press.

2. Clark, N. (1996). *Nancy Clark's sports nutrition guidebook* (2nd ed.). Champaign, IL: Human Kinetics.

Up to this point we have focused on using mental skills and viewing your body positively. All these skills directly influence your ability to reach your potential in gymnastics. There are other factors related to mental health that may seem less directly related to your gymnastics performance. One is maintaining balance in your life. Read on to understand how balance can affect your performance.

THE ROLE OF GYMNASTICS IN YOUR LIFE

After reading the previous chapters, you now have several mental skills in your arsenal. Here are a few more areas to consider as you work toward achieving your gymnastics (and life) goals. These include balancing your life, making the sport fun, and persevering in the face of obstacles.

BALANCING YOUR LIFE

"I think balance is VERY important. I went to normal high school etc. . . . Obviously I was very focused, but I had and have a life. If I wouldn't have made the Olympics, I still would've had my regular life. I never want to look back on my life and say I wish I would've."

—Amanda Borden

"I always set aside time for school, family, and friends. I feel that this helps you get away from the sport when you are not in the gym. What goes on there stays there."

—Jaycie Phelps

"It has been very important for me to balance my family, school, and gymnastics. All three are extremely important to me. It is nice to have some time when I don't have to think about gymnastics (this is at school), and I don't bring school or family into the gym with me."

—Shannon Miller

"There's a fine line. For me I needed other things to defer my attention away from the gym. I always liked Sunday to do homework, see a movie, be with my family. (Anything not pertaining to gymnastics.)"

—Kerri Strug

Your commitment to gymnastics can range from a few hours a week if you are interested in a fun physical activity to twenty or more hours a week if you have highly competitive aspirations. If gymnastics is more recreational for you, then balance is probably easy to achieve, but with the hours of training needed to reach a highly competitive level, gymnastics can take over a youngster's life. The higher the competitive level, the more time and dedication are required. Every aspect of life centers on the sport. A gymnast can literally eat, sleep, and live gymnastics. Some athletes do not even attend regular school but have tutors instead. In this way they miss out on important peer social interactions. Yet many believe the sacrifices to reach their goals are worthwhile.

In many ways these elite athletes seem like miniature adults with all their responsibilities and intense dedication, but they are still children. Some gymnasts feel they are able to maintain a childhood—they have outside friends, participate in school activities, and date. Others miss out on important parts of their childhoods and never get these opportunities until they quit the sport. Kerri Strug, for example, had many firsts after she went to college, including dating. Often, though, at highly competitive levels, there soon comes a choice point. Many gymnasts choose to drop out of the sport when they discover there is little time for other interests.

Although many gymnasts are willing to give up childhood and/or adolescent activities to reach goals they have set for themselves, these childhood opportunities can never be completely regained. There are differing opinions on whether such a sacrifice is worthwhile. It is not our purpose to determine whether such life choices are right or wrong, but rather to discuss the need to achieve some balance and how to do so.

First, it is important to realize that for high-level competitors, elite, or National team members, having complete balance is not realistic. To achieve the excellence needed at these levels requires committing a high percentage of time to training.

No matter how dedicated or driven a gymnast is, though, he or she cannot train every waking hour (or even half the waking hours!). Such a routine might produce initial positive results by increasing strength and learning new skills. Soon, though, such training will become counterproductive. Gymnasts can burn out physically and psychologically, and practices would then become less useful. There is a limit to how much time can be committed to gymnastics, and all gymnasts have to find an appropriate balance.

If a gymnast continues to compete in college, she will experience continued time demands. The hours of training may be limited because of class/student commitments and NCAA regulations, but training time still will be substantial. It may be her first time away from home with newfound independence and the first time she has to learn to balance many activities on her own. She has new opportunities for social activities and a chance to do things she has never done before. Balancing time in college continues to be a challenge.

Each gymnast will have different needs for outside activities. Some may love gymnastics and be satisfied with having all their activities revolve around the sport. Others may crave opportunities outside of gymnastics, such as time for social activities or school clubs. Balance will take on a different form for each gymnast. When creating balance, you will need to prioritize your activities and consider your feelings about each. Then determine how much of each activity you want to do and how much you realistically can do. If it is only a couple of hours a week, make that time count. Find activities you really enjoy. Those might include time with family and friends, school social functions (such as dances or football games), or trips to the movies.

It is important to develop other interests because there will be life after gymnastics. No one can be a competitive gymnast forever. For women, it is rare to compete after college. Because men tend to reach their prime in college, they might have more opportunities to compete after college, especially if they are training toward the Olympics, but most gymnasts experience a relatively early end to their careers. Often gymnasts have difficulty making the transition to non-athlete status after retiring from sport. It is helpful to have some experience with other activities under your belt to make the transition more smoothly.

Coach Jerry Tomlinson congratulating UCLA gymnast.

Coaches and parents can play a vital role in monitoring young gymnasts' activities and in making sure they find some balance. If a gymnast is completely absorbed in the sport, the adult can suggest other opportunities. Or if a gymnast begins talking about needing other activities in his or her life, adults can support those efforts. At the same time, parents and coaches need to be aware of overload from too many time commitments. These adults can monitor any stress gymnasts might feel as they try to include a variety of activities and help them prioritize. Adults must be in tune to the athlete and notice his or her behaviors, such as nervousness, irritability, preoccupation, difficulty sleeping, or complaints about physical ailments (see chapter 5 which includes symptoms of anxiety).

Most important, adults must listen very carefully to what the gymnast is communicating about his or her needs. Sometimes an athlete will clearly say something is bothering him or her. Many parents and coaches understand and respond to the athlete's needs. Sometimes, though, it is hard for parents or coaches to hear what they do not want to hear. For instance, parents might not want to hear that the athlete is becoming discouraged. Other athletes might communicate more indirectly when they attempt to share something of importance, possibly because they do not know what to say or are fearful of a parent's or coach's reaction. Therefore, parents and coaches will find it useful to set aside one-on-one time with the gymnast to reflect on how training is going and the gymnast's satisfactions and dissatisfactions. Turn off the TV or radio. Give the gymnast your undivided attention. Ask questions. Be prepared to hear the truth, not just what you hope to hear. It's no easy job being the parent or coach of a gymnast and assisting him or her in finding some balance.

Such a tremendous time commitment is not for everyone. Each gymnast should have the option of choosing NOT to do gymnastics and then pursuing other activities instead. It might be difficult for a parent or coach to watch a very talented gymnast give up the sport for some other interest. It may be tempting to talk him or her into continuing. When a parent or coach feels a great need to talk an athlete back into a sport, the adult must carefully consider whose interests are being served. Is the child doing the sport because he or she wants to? Or is the child doing the sport because the parent finds satisfaction from the child's success?

Consider this conversation:

Daughter: I am so tired of gymnastics. . . . I want to quit.

Mother: Oh, you don't want to quit . . . you are just feeling down right now.

D: No, I really want to quit. I don't like spending so much time in workouts. I miss out on talking to my friends and hanging out after school because I have to rush off to gym.

M: But just think of the scholarship you could get for college. You'll have lots of time to spend with your friends later.

D: No, Mom, I don't want to do it anymore. I don't like the pressure when competition season comes around. I want to have more fun.

M: Oh, it's just a phase you are going through. You'll come out of it and you'll thank me for not letting you quit.

D: No, I've thought about it and it's not worth it.

M: Stay in a little longer; I'm sure you'll get over it. You just have to set your mind to it.

So back the daughter trudges to the gym. She is unmotivated, uncooperative, and unhappy. The coach becomes frustrated with her, and the child feels even worse.

The daughter is clearly communicating her need to reprioritize her life—in fact, she says the same thing four times!—but the mother is not listening. As we discussed in the chapter on parental influences, parents have a very powerful role in helping their gymnasts choose a sport path. Parents also have the responsibility to put aside their own wishes and help the gymnast make decision with which she or he will be comfortable.

After reading this chapter, you might be thinking about your own situation. If you are wondering who is getting what from gymnastics, think about the following questions:

- Why is the gymnast doing gymnastics?

- What does he or she get out of gymnastics?

- What would it mean if he or she gave up gymnastics?

- What does the parent or coach get out of gymnastics?

- What would it mean for the parent/coach if the gymnast gave up gymnastics?

As you look at the answers, determine who seems more motivated for the gymnast to continue. If it is the gymnast, then parents can continue to support the athlete in reaching his or her goals. If it seems that the parent/coach is more motivated than the child, then it is time to examine those motives. Although it might be difficult for an adult to watch the child quit, it may be in the child's best interest.

If you maintain balance you are more likely to enjoy your life and all the opportunities you have. Having a variety of interests also can make gymnastics more enjoyable. Sometimes, though, we have to consciously remember to keep the fun in the sport. The next chapter offers some ideas for keeping the fun alive.

28

KEEPING FUN IN THE GYMNASTICS GAME

"The most important thing is to have fun. If you are enjoying something you will want to work hard at it, and therefore, you will be the best you can be."

—Amanda Borden

Case: Alicia stood in front of the bars and stared. She had been working on this routine all season and still could not get it right. Her hands were sore, her muscles ached, and she was so tired. She remembered when she first began gymnastics. She could not wait to get to the gym; bars was her favorite event. She remembered the first time she got the swing and rhythm of a kip and the sense of accomplishment. She would hurry home each day and tell her parents what new skill she had learned. Now it was a chore. The excitement had worn off long ago, and she was trying to determine why she continued to train so hard. Something was missing. What had happened?

Fun means different things to different people at different points in their lives. However you define fun for yourself, it is a very important concept for gymnastics. Most gymnasts begin gymnastics lessons because they are fun. They love the sensations and movements, the chance to toss themselves in the air and land on their feet (usually). When gymnasts learn new things, they feel a sense of accomplishment. When they perform well, there is recognition. Developing friendships and "hanging out" with other athletes are other rewarding parts of being involved in gymnastics. All of these things can be fun and are reasons gymnasts remain in the sport. As training progresses and commitment increases, however, seriousness can invade. Gymnastics is hard work, and progress sometimes seems slow. Athletes can lose confidence, suffer injuries, feel pressures to be involved in other activities, and experience disappointments. The enjoyment may become fleeting, or maybe it is gone altogether.

If you are struggling to find the fun in gymnastics, get a pen or pencil and some paper, and do Exercise 25-1.

28-1: HAVING FUN

1. Assess whom you are doing the sport for. Is it truly for you, or is it because of pressures from a parent or coach? Are you training and competing only for the momentary recognition that comes from a good meet? Do you feel pressured to keep going to get a college scholarship? On your paper make a list of the reason(s) you are doing gymnastics.

   Now look at those reasons. If you are doing the sport for someone or something else besides your own satisfaction, you may find fun more difficult to come by.

2. Next, determine what you used to enjoy about gymnastics. What was it about gymnastics that you loved? How did you get involved at first? Remember those times that made you enjoy the sport. Make a second list of what you enjoy or have enjoyed about gymnastics.

3. Now look at how much you currently enjoy gymnastics. When you compare it to the enjoyable times, what is missing? Make a third list of what is currently missing for you. Also think about what is fun for you now (this may be different than what was fun when you began the sport) and how that could be a part of gymnastics. Begin thinking about how you can put some of the fun back into gymnastics.

If you continue to have fun, then hold onto it! Use the following strategies to keep it that way. If you are struggling to have fun, then read on to learn how to incorporate more fun into the sport.

1. Talk to your coach. If you are comfortable with your coach, have an honest, heart-to-heart conversation about what is bothering you. Maybe the coach has some ideas about how to make training more fun.

2. Change your thinking. If you go into workouts with a negative attitude ("I am so tired today," "I don't want to be here," or "I'm going to have a bad workout"), nothing is going to be fun. Talk yourself into having fun by finding parts of the workout you enjoy and focusing on them.

3. Change your routine. Not necessarily your gymnastics routines, but the order in which you do things. Sometimes it is easy to get into a monotonous routine, the same things every day. That can bore anyone. Find ways to make workouts more exciting. Again, ask your coach for ideas here.

4. Make sure gymnastics provides you with the appropriate amount of challenge. Gymnastics needs to be challenging but not too challenging. If it isn't challenging enough for your skills, you might feel bored; if it is too challenging, you might feel stressed. Either way you wouldn't have much fun. So try to match your goals with your skills so that you have an optimal amount of challenge.

5. Find time for other, non-gymnastics activities. If your whole focus is on gymnastics, it can lose its appeal. You may need the variety in your life. Gymnastics may become more enjoyable if it is one of many activities.

If you try, and really make an effort, to put the fun back into gymnastics, and it still is not fun, consider taking a break. Not everyone thrives in the hard-working, competitive gymnastics environment. If you truly have lost the fun, consider finding other activities that bring you more enjoyment.

29

CONCLUSION: STAYING TOUGH IN THE FACE OF DISAPPOINTMENTS

We hope that you now have a better understanding of the psychology of gymnastics. Many sport psychology skills have been presented throughout this book as well as mental strategies for dealing the issues you might face in gymnastics. Practice to make these skills permanent.

We realize, though, that even the best gymnasts will face disappointments during their gymnastics careers. It might be a fall that knocks the athlete out of an important competition, an "off day" that also just happens to be the day of an important meet, frustration when learning new skills seems slow, or losing a skill.

It is important to remember that no matter how well prepared you are, both physically and mentally, disappointments will occur; there is no way around that. Sometimes it is tempting to give up, but if you really love gymnastics and want to reach your goals, you have to work through the disappointments. Remember that some of the most important work is done during the hardest times.

Even Olympic champions can remember disappointing points in their careers:

> Amanda Borden: "'92 Olympic trials made me a much better and stronger athlete. I just barely missed the team and went through a really tough time. I almost quit! It made me realize why I was doing gym. I loved the sport and came back even stronger four years later."

> Jaycie Phelps: "American Cup—I fell apart, missed three out of four events. I was hurt and didn't get to prepare enough. I learned that every gymnast trains different(ly) and I am the type that needs lots of numbers. That is why I am where I am today."

> Kerri Strug: "Classics '94 Palm Springs. I fell and stress fractured my back. Initially I wanted to give up but after a few days I was more determined to come back. It made me realize anything can happen but you can't give up on your dreams."

After reading about these experiences, you can probably remember some disappointments of your own. Learn from these champions, and recognize that with perseverance and hard work you can get past disappointments too. Focus on your dreams, train hard physically, and use your mental toughness skills that you have learned in this book to help you be the best gymnast and person you can be. All the best to you in every part of your life!

REFERENCES

AAUW. (1991). *Shortchanging girls, shortchanging America*. Washington, DC: American Association of University Women.

American College of Sports Medicine Position Stand on the Female Athlete Triad. *Medicine and Science in Sports and Exercies, 29*, i–ix.

The American Heritage College Dictionary, Third Edition (1993). Boston, MA: Houghton Mifflin Company.

American Psychiatric Association. (1994). *Diagnostic and statistical manual of mental disorders* (4th ed.). Washington, DC: Author.

Feltz, D. L., & Landers, D. M. (1983). The effects of mental practice on motor skill learning and performance: A meta-analysis. *Journal of Sport Psychology, 5*, 25–57.

Gould, D., & Damarjian, N. (1996). Imagery training for peak performance. In J. L. Van Raalte & B. W. Brewer (Eds.), *Exploring sport and exercise psychology* (pp. 25–50). Washington, DC: American Psychological Association.

International Gymnast (1994). *Christy Henrich. 1972–94*. Pg. 48–49

Nideffer, R. M. (1986). Concentration and attention control training. In J. M. Williams (Ed.), *Applied sport psychology: Personal growth to peak performance* (pp. 257–269). Palo Alto, CA: Mayfield Publishing Company.

Petrie, T. A. (1993). Disordered eating in female collegiate gymnasts: Prevalence and personality/attitudinal correlates. *Journal of Sport & Exercise Psychology, 15*, 424–436.

Petrie, T. A., & Stoever, S. (1993). The incidence of bulimia nervosa and pathogenic weight control behaviors in female collegiate gymnasts. *Research Quarterly for Exercise and Sport, 64*, 238–241.

Streigel-Moore, R., Silberstein, L., & Rodin, J. (1986). Toward an understanding of risk factors for bulimia. *American Psychologist, 41*, 246–263.

Weinberg, R. S. (1996). Goal setting in sport and exercise: Research to practice. In J. L. Van Raalte & B. W. Brewer (Eds.), *Exploring sport and exercise psychology* (pp. 3–24). Washington, DC: American Psychological Association.

Williams, J. W., & Leffingwell, T. R. (1996). Cognitive strategies in sport and exercise psychology. In J. L. Van Raalte & B. W. Brewer (Eds.), *Exploring Sport and Exercise Psychology* (pp. 51–74). Washington, DC: American Psychological Association.

INDEX

GLOSSARY OF TERMS

Delchev: Release with half turn, then straddled front salto to regrasp.

Fly away: A dismount on bars coming often coming out of a handstand on high bar or giant swing. At the bottom of the swing, the gymnast lets go of the bar and flips to land on feet.

Full in: A double back flip with a full twist on the first flip.

Full in/full out: A double back flip with a full twist on each flip.

Gainer layout: A one-legged takeoff layout with the other foot swinging to begin the backward rotation.

Gaylord flip: Named for Mitch Gaylord; starts as a front giant and as the gymnast comes up over the bar, he or she releases and does a 1 1/2 flip over the high bar.

Giant: A basic swing skill on bars. While holding the high bar, the gymnast swings completely around (up and over) the bar with a straight body.

Gienger: Piked flyaway with half turn to regrasp.

Handstand: Balance upside down on hands with feet up in the air; a basic gymnastics skill on which many other skills build.

Layout: A back flip in a straight body position.